MARTHA BRETTSCHNEIDER

Blooming INTO Mindfulness

How the Universe Used a Garden,

Cancer, and Carpools to Teach Me That

Calm Is the New Happy

DAMSELWINGS PRESS

DAMSELWINGS
PRESS

Published by Damselwings Press
Vienna, Virginia
www.damselwingspress.com

Publisher's Cataloging-In-Publication Data
(Prepared by The Donohue Group, Inc.)

Brettschneider, Martha.
  Blooming into mindfulness : how the universe used a garden, cancer, and carpools to teach me that calm is the new happy / Martha Brettschneider.
-- First edition.

    pages : illustrations ; cm

Issued also as an ebook.
Includes bibliographical references.
ISBN: 978-0-9969352-0-3 (hardcopy)
ISBN: 978-0-9969352-2-7 (paperback)

1. Brettschneider, Martha. 2. Mindfulness (Psychology) 3. Peace of mind. 4. Women economists--Psychology. 5. Breast--Cancer--Patients--Psychology. 6. Mothers--Psychology. 7. Gardening--Therapeutic use. I. Title.

BF637.P3 B74 2016
158.1   2015918842

Printed in the United States of America

For my mother, who taught me to bloom bravely.

Table of Contents

Introduction

I have a pair of blue denim overalls.

The overalls are faded and the knees are stained with two decades' worth of weeding and planting. A few paint splatters adorn the left leg. The hardware that holds the straps in place is tired, allowing for one strap or the other to slip off my shoulder with great regularity. The right hip button comes undone easily, exposing the side of my underpants.

Sometimes I readjust the straps; sometimes I reclose the button. But because my hands are encased in dirt-covered gardening gloves when I'm wearing my overalls, I usually let these wardrobe failures slide.

The overalls are my version of a church lady's Sunday hat. I wear them when I'm entering my most peaceful place. I wear them when I'm connecting with a higher power. I wear them when I want to hear what my heart has to say. For me, gardening provides a portal to calm. Gardening connects me to the rest of creation.

But this isn't a gardening book.

My garden does, indeed, play a lead role in the story told here. I credit her (yes, I think of my garden as a "her") with slapping me upside the head as a young, career-driven, stressed-out mom, admonishing me to simmer down, shut up, and go out and grow something.

Your story may feature another character in the lead role. It could be painting, writing, photography, or jewelry making. It could be horseback riding, scuba diving, running, walking in the woods, or simply sitting on a park bench and watching the clouds roll by.

This book is about how my garden sparked a process of transformation that life events subsequently deepened and accelerated. I had never planned on having a garden. I had never planned on most of the life events that shaped me.

I spent the first couple of decades of adulthood resisting the reality of my life, which to any outside observer was pretty great. The internal narrator in my head, however, always had to look for something to complain about. My own thinking process was my greatest source of suffering.

The garden grounded me. While cultivating the soil, thoughts about what I "should" be doing with my life instead of raising kids or how I "should" be using that master's degree dissolved. The scent of the loamy earth cleared my head. The life force in a root ball was palpable in my hands. A glint of sunlight reflecting off an earthworm drew my attention to even tinier creatures digging in the dirt alongside me. The sensory experience of gardening silenced the crazy-making voice in my head, replacing the whiny chatter with a deep (and quite unfamiliar) sense of peace.

The garden was my first mindfulness mentor, but I didn't know it at the time.

Mindfulness—the practice of paying attention to the present moment and observing one's thoughts nonjudgmentally, without getting carried away by past or future stories—is bandied about frequently these days. The term is often paired with the ever-growing body of neuroscience findings on the health benefits of meditation.

But when I first met my garden over twenty years ago, I had never heard of mindfulness, let alone practiced it. Meditation in those days was still the purview of spiritual seekers and crystal-carrying hippie types. I was a left-brained international economist above all of that nonsense. I had more important things to do.

The problem was, the garden could only work her magic when I was physically in her embrace. The rest of the time I was still a prisoner to my internal bully, that voice in my head that told me I wasn't living up to society's expectations of me, wasn't doing important enough work, wasn't making enough money, and wasn't appreciated enough by my family for all that I had sacrificed for them. My internal bully made me suffer, but I didn't even recognize it as suffering since that state of mind was my norm. I think that's the case for many of us.

This is a story about how I learned to recognize that the internal bully is not my true self. My true self, it turns out, is quite a bit different from the person I had thought I was supposed to be. Though it took me a while to accept her, my true self is a lot more enjoyable to be around, both for me and everyone else in my life. My true self reached a negotiated settlement with that ugly internal bully, who now keeps quiet most of the time.

Twists and turns have marked the journey, many of them amusing, others not so much. Breast cancer barged into my life in 2009, shoving the garden to the side and forcing me to clear my perennially crowded calendar for a year of treatment and recovery. An accidental download of an audiobook led to an epiphany. Many teachers crossed my path without my actively seeking them. Through it all, the garden was always in the background, welcoming me when I had time for her, forgiving me when I didn't, never ever judging me.

The story is presented in three parts. Part I, "Dormant," paints a picture of my pre-awareness life. Chaos, resistance, and constant battles with ego dominated this period, in line with the *American Heritage Dictionary* definition of dormant as "cessation of growth or development." Despite my busyness as a young mother, I was dormant in the midst of the frenzy.

Part II, "Pruned," introduces my breast cancer experience and its role in catalyzing a complete reorientation of my body, mind, and spirit. Though a piece of my body was indeed "removed or cut out," in line with the dictionary definition of "pruned," many parts of my life were also pruned back during this period. Pruning a plant directs energy back down to the roots, strengthening prospects for future growth. There is no better analogy than this for the role breast cancer played in my life. This section culminates with a spiritual epiphany in the garden that literally made me drop my trowel.

Part III, "Blossoming," describes the practical steps I took to learn to listen more closely to my heart and embrace my true self—to "develop" and "flourish," as it were. Strengthening my body (per my cancer team's orders), creating a living environment that enhanced positive energy flows, and eventually training my mind through a structured program of daily meditation were all essential ingredients to nurturing my best self.

You will meet the teachers who were instrumental in my journey. I write about them with great enthusiasm, but I am not a paid advertiser for anyone. Your teachers will likely be different, as each and every one of us brings a unique history to the table that determines how we process language and open ourselves to new possibilities.

Though the details of my journey and teachers are distinct to me, I believe the lessons are universal. Identity struggles, conflicting demands of parenting and career, full satisfaction always just a little out of reach, the life-altering impact of serious illness, the quest for purpose—these are common challenges that many (if not most) people face. Anne Lamott once said, "As writers, I think we need to be part of the solution." It's in the spirit of that call to action that I wrote this book.

My story attests that if we train ourselves to access the deeper intelligence below our surface brain chatter and have the courage to take purposeful action based on our heart's wisdom, we can emerge stronger, more joyful, and more content than we could ever have imagined.

PART I

Dormant

dormant: *adj.* 1. Lying asleep or as if asleep; inactive. 2. Latent but capable of being activated . . . 3. Temporarily quiescent . . . 4. In a condition of biological rest or inactivity characterized by cessation of growth or development and the suspension of many metabolic processes . . .

—*The American Heritage Dictionary of the English Language,* fourth edition

CHAPTER 1

Welcome to the Suburbs

The suburbs were never part of the plan.

Navigating my way through the equivalent of *Mister Rogers' Neighborhood* on a bright May afternoon in 1994, all I could think was, *Oh, god. How did this happen? Did I really just buy a house in the suburbs? Am I really going to live here in just a few weeks?* My stomach tightened at the thought of it.

Even though I had been to the house three or four times already, I still hadn't memorized how to get there. My incapacity to remember this route was exacerbated by denial about my impending life transition. "GPS" was still an undiscovered acronym then. I didn't own a cell phone. MapQuest and Google Maps hadn't been born yet. All I had to guide me was my barely legible penmanship scrawled on a ragged piece of paper, now clenched between my clammy palm and the steering wheel.

Double-checking my scribbles while pulling onto the street of my final destination, I turned into the second driveway on the left. The Sold sign swung from its hinges on the realtor's signpost. I stopped the engine and yanked the emergency brake lever skyward. I'd always liked the wrench of emergency brakes engaging—the sound and feel of control. The sensation comforted me even more on the steep slope of this driveway, where I instinctively felt out of my element.

I looked up at the white brick colonial perched on the hill. It did look stately, with its gleaming black shutters, red door, and ridged columns flanking the portico. But I hadn't set out on this journey looking for stately. I had been perfectly content without stately.

My pale-green silk suit, crumpled from the thirty-minute drive from my office in Washington, D.C., caught the sunlight as I stepped out of the car. My nylons dug into my waist, reminding me how much worse it would be when the Virginia humidity arrived in a few months. I had to admit that it did feel cooler and somehow fresher out here. I ran my fingers through my hair, both to smooth it out after driving with the windows open and to dry my hands. Sweaty palms had become a Pavlovian response to crossing over the Capital Beltway two miles back.

I had left work early to meet my fiancé here. *At our house.* I had to get used to saying that. We had signed the contract but hadn't moved in yet. *I live in Vienna, Virginia.* I had to get used to saying that too. My palms started to sweat all over again. Just a few short months ago, the only thing I knew about Vienna, Virginia, was that it had a good Turkish restaurant. The friend who brought me there had said, "This is the only reason I would ever come all the way out to Vienna."

Standing next to my tiny, slightly battered Toyota Starlet, the house seemed enormous to me. With 2,300 square feet of living space, it was about four times bigger than my cozy studio apartment in Washington, D.C. I felt as if I were moving into *Gone with the Wind's* Tara.

Did I mention before that I hadn't been yearning for Tara? I loved living in the heart of the nation's capital. I had moved to Washington's Dupont Circle three years earlier, after landing a job as an international economist at the U.S. Treasury Department. Having scraped through graduate school on financial fumes, often resorting to stocking up on free saltines at the soup counter, I was finally earning enough not only to live on my own, but to make my student loan payments as well. Just barely, mind you, but after remembering all too clearly the days when my checking account often lacked the $10 minimum required for an ATM withdrawal, I felt I could finally exhale.

And exhale I did as I lowered myself into my tiny bathroom's claw-foot tub each night, resting a plate of spaghetti tossed with olive oil, garlic, and parmesan cheese on my chest to nibble at my leisure, a fork in one hand, a book in the other, a lit candle and glass of wine perched on top of the closed toilet lid. Heaven and decadence rolled into one, and all of it legal. I didn't need another inch of space.

Having served my time as a responsible roommate for a decade, sharing dorms, apartments, and houses in four states and two foreign countries since graduating from high school, I reveled in the luxury of a room of my own. Nobody else's comfort mattered any more. Clothes lay heaped in piles for days; dishes grew moldy in the sink during business trips; books, CDs, and papers littered the floor until I invited someone over and felt compelled to cover up my secret pigpen ways. Because the studio was so small, it never took long to clean up. And without a pet or even a houseplant to care for, travel for work—to locales as far flung as Seoul, Geneva, or Paris, just to name a few—or for play required nothing more than an airline ticket or a full tank of gas.

Walking to work each day, the city slapped my senses awake. It didn't matter if it was Washington, Seattle, Istanbul, or West Berlin. I had lived and worked in all of these cities and traveled through dozens more. Cabs honking, the morning sun reflecting off glass-wrapped office buildings, street performers making music and mayhem in pedestrian zones and subway stations, flowers blasting color from the vendor's buckets of blooms, and all manner of food aromas taunting my taste buds.

The suburbs could never compete. While a lot of girls dream of the day they'll get married and move into a big house with a white picket fence, I hadn't been one of them. For one thing, I knew firsthand that tidy front yards in cookie-cutter neighborhoods were no indication of tidy lives behind the front doors.

My own family had moved from suburb to suburb, five times during my first nine years of childhood. Despite the promise of a fresh start in each new neighborhood, and no matter how pretty the new digs may have been, the suburbs did not translate into emotional security, at least for me.

My mother did a yeoman's job of giving us the outside trappings of the American dream—sending us to good schools, managing PTA activities, carpooling for sports teams, leading Camp Fire Girls troops, and piling plenty of gifts around the Christmas tree. To the outside world, my two older sisters and I were the well-kept children of a successful transplant surgeon. I used to tell anyone who would listen that my father's hands had been on the cover of *Life* magazine in the late 1960s as part of the team that conducted the first liver and kidney transplants. But inside our suburban walls, my father's bipolar disorder-induced demons tore our family apart. It was inside yet another pretty suburban home, the one he shared with his new wife after my parents divorced, that he took his own life a few days after my thirteenth birthday.

So let's just say I had trust issues with the suburbs, not to mention trust issues with marriage in general.

But here I was, standing on the front lawn of a house in which my own family might have once lived, wondering how I had lost control of the reins.

When Mark and I met, I boasted that when I filled out my first security clearance application, I had eighteen addresses to report over the previous fifteen years, many of them overseas. And that didn't even include the early moves with my family. Mark had just returned from a two-year stint in Africa and had lived in Rio de Janeiro twice as a child while his father served at the U.S. embassy there. Mark was not intimidated by my past, or by my hopes for the future. The songs we eventually chose for our wedding were about travel and adventure and not needing to settle down in one place to be happy. "Wherever we're together, that's my home" was my favorite line in the Billy Joel song we'd selected.

It was true, when we embarked on our house search soon after becoming engaged, that I had said I didn't want a tiny starter home. Mark was thirty-five, I was thirty (a "mature bride," according to the bridal shop saleswoman), and we hoped to start a family sooner rather than later. I loved children and had always envisioned having kids of my own, even while questioning whether a cost-benefit analysis of marriage worked out in its favor. Mark's patient steadiness, his yin to my yang, finally tipped the scales for me, convincing me that one plus one in our case added up to more than two.

When we started our house search, I had several requirements.

Condition number 1: The place had to be big enough to accommodate the still-theoretical baby or two, as well as the very real parrots (two of them) and cats (again, two of them) that Mark brought to the marriage from the outset. My mother's Herculean efforts to move our family from place to place in my early years were etched deeply in my memory. It was one thing to transport myself and my few possessions to a new space—I was a pro at that by now. But I knew it was quite another to move kids and dishes and furniture and pets and books and TVs, and everything else that filled those boxes I had helped pack and unpack over and over again as a kid.

The good news was that, just as we started our search, a large international financial institution offered me a position that would more than double my salary. My paycheck was bigger than Mark's now, a fact that I bandied about wherever possible (and still look back on with some nostalgia).

Condition number 2: The house had to be inside the Capital Beltway, I insisted, since I was sure that none of my friends would visit us if we were further out. The so-called Beltway is Interstate 495, the sixty-four-mile-long highway that circles Washington and its suburbs in Maryland and Virginia. An import from the Pacific Northwest, I had been told by my D.C. friends that the Beltway served as the dividing line between civilization and the boonies. And this was even more true in Virginia, they had warned, the state on the wrong side of the Civil War.

Condition number 3: The house had to have enough natural light coming through the windows to offset my seasonal depression. Sunlight was a mood booster that I had come to depend on, even while feeling like a traitor to my beloved Seattle by admitting it. I needed any and all tools at my disposal if I was going to be waking up in the suburbs every morning. Like George Bailey throwing a lasso around the moon, my house would need to lasso the sun.

Mark's conditions were good schools, a good value, and, preferably, a location in Virginia, where his family was based.

"Let's just see what's out there," he said with a degree of calm that I was beginning to find annoying.

So we set out on our house-hunting journey with our cheerful real estate agent, starting close to the city at my request and slowly making a circular route into Maryland, back over to Virginia, back into Maryland, and back into Virginia. I rejected house after house as being either too small or too dark. In some cases the schools were an issue.

It quickly became clear that our budget wouldn't take us very far within the confines of the Beltway. Mark remained patient, with not a single "I told you so."

Even if the house was big enough (I didn't want a McMansion—I just wanted a few bedrooms and a dining room for dinner parties to lure our friends over with food), the older neighborhoods close to the city felt cramped and shady. The mature trees were lovely in principle, but the light deficit would have turned me into Stephen King's family-killing protagonist in *The Shining*.

The real estate agent's smile became more forced after the thirtieth house. After the fortieth, she took longer and longer to return our calls.

"What about Vienna?" Mark said. He had suggested this very early on in the process, but my friend's disparaging remarks about Vienna, or at least its location—a whole two miles outside the Beltway on the Virginia side—were emblazoned in my memory and I had instantly nixed it.

But after rejecting house number fifty, I finally agreed to loosen my grip on the geographic constraints. The wedding was just a few months away, and we planned to squeeze in a housewarming party as the first event of our wedding weekend. Time was running out.

Relieved to have a little more leeway, the real estate agent called and said, "I have something I think you'll like."

A breeze nudged the Sold sign into squeaky motion, pulling me back to the present. Mark and I now owned this house. He would be meeting me here in a few minutes with the keys so that we could walk through and decide what work needed to be done before we moved in.

A flash of movement in the side yard caught my eye, and I turned to discover a freckled, auburn-haired little girl watching me, grinning broadly.

"Are you coming from church?" she asked.

Remembering it was Wednesday, I thought, *Great. My neighbors are fundamentalist Christians who go to church every day of the week.*

I wondered what they would think if they knew that, just a week earlier, I had negotiated most mentions of God out of the draft wedding ceremony the rabbi had shown us, as well as every single reference to God's maleness.

So, no, I wasn't coming from church.

"I'm coming from work," I replied.

"Do you have kids?" she asked, without missing a beat.

"No," I said. "We're not quite married yet. Our wedding's in a few months, though, in October."

A woman, the girl's mother no doubt, was approaching from the house next door, probably horrified that I was corrupting her young daughter with my confession that we'd be living in sin before our wedding. My high heels sank into the grass.

"Hi, I'm Diane," the woman said, pulling off her gardening glove to shake my hand. "And this is Katy." Her friendly eyes and warm smile threw me off guard. It had taken only a nanosecond to assume I'd have Mrs. Kravitz (the nosy, wicked next-door neighbor from the old TV show *Bewitched*) living in the house next to mine. It would have been more fun to think so, since villains always make for a better story. But I could tell in an instant that I would like Diane.

"She's not coming from church, Mom. She's coming from *work*," Katy announced.

"I used to have a life too, you know," Diane said with a wry smile, ruffling Katy's hair.

My shoulders relaxed with the realization that I wasn't being judged. I slipped out of my shoes, dislodging the impaled heels. Two deep punctures stared up at me from the earth.

"When you have babies, can I babysit?" Katy asked.

"Excuse me?" It was all I could come up with.

"Can I babysit? When you have babies?"

"Oh. Um, sure. I guess. How old are you?"

"Eight," she said, with as much authority as any interviewee for a corporate job.

"Okay," I said, "but can we just get through the wedding first before we talk about babies?"

Meeting the Garden

A garden was never part of the plan.

To my untrained eye, our new house's landscape was fine. More than fine, in fact. The owners had timed the sale perfectly to coincide with the blooming of the mature Bradford pear trees that lined both sides of the street as far as the eye could see. The first time we saw the property, Mark and I exclaimed "Oooooh!" in unison at the sight of the frothy white explosion of blossoms.

Three dogwood trees served as backup performers to the Bradfords. Azaleas planted in a red, white, red, white pattern along the front walkway made a perky—if patriotic—display, daffodils bobbed their yellow heads in the breeze, and a sumptuously fragrant lilac bush adorned the corner of the carport. Behind the house, an ornamental cherry tree was preparing to burst into flower at any moment.

Totally ignorant of all things garden-related, I filed this image in my head with the label "This Is What My Yard Will Always Look Like." Colorful flowers would bloom all year long, the cherry tree would stay the same size, the Bradfords would remain intact during wind storms.

I knew nothing at that point about Bradfords, which have short life spans, weak joints, and give off a stench of rotten eggs at the height of their blossom time. The tree odor was crowded out of our senses on that first visit by the sparkling white house behind the For Sale sign.

The fact that absolutely no flat space existed on the plot, with the exception of the small brick patio behind the house, should have at least been noted. Even if I had known at that point that we would be blessed with two wildly athletic boys who could have used some level ground to kick a soccer ball around, I had never stayed in one place long enough to take future home-based scenarios into consideration.

Gardening experience, or even the slightest interest in trying to plant something one day, might also have led to a more critical assessment of the property. But I wasn't a gardener. This was true in every possible respect. I could have borne the label, at least, if I had taken Mark's last name when we married—it happens to be Gardiner (with an "i").

But I chose to keep my own complicated last name. It had taken me long enough to learn how to spell Brettschneider, and it was already printed on my business cards. On top of that, I was probably the last of my family's lineage, unless the uncle who ran away as a teenager in the 1950s had children I didn't know about. Finally, I knew women who had gone through two or three husbands, changing their name each time. As an economist, I found that highly inefficient. Mark didn't have an issue with me keeping my name, so it was never a point of contention. I was a gardener in neither name nor deed.

If you ask most gardeners what inspired them to pick up the trowel, they'll probably tell you about the gardens of their youth. They'll remember plucking bosomy red orbs from their father's tomato plants. They'll remember thinking their mother's bearded irises were sticking their tongues out. They'll remember the confusing mix of intoxicating fragrance and hazardous thorniness in their grandmother's rose garden. That wasn't the case for me.

My mother was a world-class weeder, but not the garden variety. Before each of our many transitions, she would announce, "It's time to weed out!" A garage sale preceded every move, and we would shed our collective crap like a snakeskin before heading to our next new start.

My father—the Jewish kid from Brooklyn—never grew tomatoes. It could be argued, I suppose, that moving organs from one person's body to another's is just a different form of planting. And he did use gloves in his work, so there's another similarity. But my clearest memory of my father in the yard is of him doubled over in pain after throwing his back out pulling the lawn mower's starter cord.

Most of the time he left the mowing to my mother, who swore it was one of her most relaxing tasks. There was something about the ruler-straight parallel lines in the grass she created while mowing that gave at least an impression of order in our lives. But the lines always disappeared as soon as it rained.

My mother was the only woman I ever saw cutting the grass in my early years. My friends' mothers seemed weak in comparison. She always said her favorite gift from my father was the self-propelled Toro mower he gave her for Mother's Day in 1969. "Yard work" (raking leaves and digging out dandelions to improve the lawn) was a regular part of our Saturday morning chores, but "gardening" was never part of my childhood vocabulary.

In my early twenties, however, I stumbled upon a passion for flowers while studying and working in Germany. What drew me in first were European ivy geraniums gushing red and pink fountains of color under window frames and over balcony railings. More flowers moved through the streets in the arms of people bringing bouquets to dinner party hostesses, or to friends and colleagues on birthdays. Flower vendors were as essential as bakers or bankers.

The German flower ladies fascinated me, with their rough demeanors and well-padded physiques, like sturdy trees behind rows of buckets at the *Blumenstand*. You simply named your budget and perhaps pointed to one or two flowers among the many options on display, and the flower *Frau* would proceed to build a masterpiece of color, form, and fragrance. Lilies, daffodils, zinnias, dahlias, irises, poppies, tulips, delphinium—the choices went on and on. Don't forget the foxgloves, gladiolas, hydrangeas, roses, daisies, stock, nasturtia, and lisianthus. It was all there in every shade of purple, yellow, orange, red, and pink.

I learned that throwing a little white into the mix served to rest the eye and make the other colors pop that much more. I learned that greens and long viney accents provided depth and structure. I learned that a yard's worth of cellophane and a satin ribbon was like fairy dust that made the bouquet sing. I would never know all the German names for the flowers—I didn't even know the English names for most of them at that point—but I got by with pointing and asking for *die da* and *diese hier* ("that one there" and "these here"). Carnations never seemed to be an option, which accounts for my relegating them to second-class citizen status, even to this day.

Flowers became a distraction. While reading Franz Kafka or Thomas Mann or another of their heavy-hearted counterparts in a West Berlin coffee shop, flowers across the street would catch my eye and start to call until, not being able to stand it any longer, I'd pay for my cappuccino and pull on my black wool coat, the outermost of several dark layers I wore most days during that chapter of my life.

With as much magic as any Brothers Grimm fable offers, flowers cut through my crap. Carrying a bouquet brightened my spirit, lightened my baggage, and always looked great against my black wardrobe. And although I felt a twinge of sadness to let the bouquet go, seeing the recipient's face light up at the sight of their flowers left me smiling right along with them. Of course, sometimes I just kept the bundle for myself.

A couple of decades later, I would hear a mindfulness teacher point out that blue sky is always there behind the clouds. Flowers were laser beams cutting holes through my gray skies, both real and imagined.

It was one thing to buy flowers, but quite another to grow your own. Before I got married, I had been a certified nomad.

Nomads are not trained to think in terms of growing cycles and seasons and sun angles. Nomads have no vision for gardening, because they won't be around when it comes time to water or weed or harvest. Nomads have no understanding of or shared experience with perennial plants, which come back year after year in the same spot.

The first few months in our house were consumed with long workdays, wedding planning, and the time and expense of settling into home ownership. Meanwhile, my neighbor Diane worked quietly away in her garden next door. I'd come home from work and catch a glimpse of her snipping peonies, daisies, purple coneflowers, or parsley. Her hydrangeas were especially magnificent, providing an abundance of frothy blue blossoms that filled vases in her kitchen and provided rich color and texture to her backyard all summer long. As I watched her harvest her treasures, I couldn't shake the feeling that Diane was part of some magical process. It was the gardening equivalent of "I'll have what she's having."

I looked out my kitchen window into my own backyard. The rectangle of uneven brick that constituted our patio was adorned with a single pink azalea bush plopped at each corner, like dots marking the start and end points of plumb lines. The cherry tree had indeed taken my breath away during its bloom time in May, but by June the pink petals had fallen to their death and dissolved into the lawn. After the spring show that had given the place such great curb appeal during our house search, it became clear that once summer began, the party was over.

Gardening catalogs arrived unsolicited on our doorstep, part of the onslaught of advertising targeting new homeowners. Fields of flowers of my choosing were promised if only I ordered before supplies ran out.

Leafing through the pages of color-enhanced photos, nostalgia for my visits to the German flower ladies enveloped me. *Maybe I could grow some flowers of my own.* I was getting bolder with do-it-yourself projects inside the house. Why couldn't I do the same outside? The pretty catalog certainly made it look easy. For only $19.99, I could get a Jumbo Sun Perennial Grab Bag that would grow into an English cottage garden in no time.

It seemed that all I needed was a relatively flat spot with at least six hours of sun. Shouldn't be too hard to find, right? But ten-hour workdays and weekends crammed with errands made it tough to track sun patterns. I had never had a reason to stay home simply to observe what was happening at the spot where I was living. "Living" for me, at that point, meant working and planning fun excursions. Excitement was always someplace else. Home was simply where I kept my clothes and planned trips.

But the catalogs kept calling. Although I tried to keep my attention focused on whatever article I should have been reading in *The Economist,* I would invariably switch it out for flower pictures. So one weekend, I finally forced myself to stay put for a whole day with the sole purpose of locating a spot in my yard that got at least six hours of sun. Taking into consideration how those light patterns changed with the seasons and over time would have been an advanced move had I been informed enough to consider it. Just staying home was hard enough.

On paper, I had a perfect rectangle of a plot to work with—128 feet long (from front to back) and 82 feet wide (from side to side). The house was built almost exactly in the center of the rectangle, leaving 11 feet of space from the house to the property line on the left side and 9 feet of space from the edge of the carport to the property line on the right side. The sun rose over the back left corner of the plot and set over the front right corner, giving the backyard a slightly off-kilter southwest exposure.

While the length and width of the property were comprehensible in their symmetry, the third dimension was the kicker. The topography of our little piece of earth was as wavy as a blanket having the dust shaken out of it. The "house on the hill" impression I'd had when we bought the place turned out to be too simple a label. The house was embedded in the

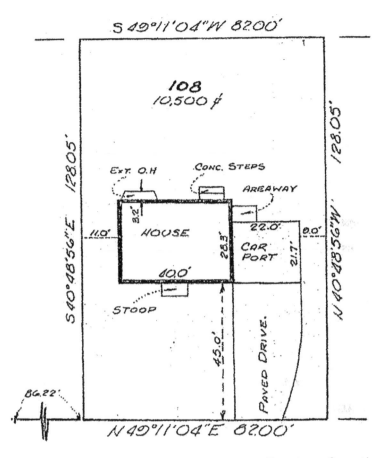

side of a hill, with slopes running in every direction—from the sidewalk up to the front of the house, from the back patio up to the back property line, with a less drastic but still significant slope running downward from the right side of the property to the left side.

Tall trees spanned the length of the back property line, creating more shade than my imagined flower garden could tolerate. My library books told me that cutting gardens (which seemed to be the type of garden I would need if I were to replicate the German flower ladies' bouquets) could get scraggly looking, so the front yard was out. I settled on a spot for a small raised bed along the west side of the backyard fence, with one end flush with the slope and the other end (only 97 inches away) raised a foot to create a level planting bed about four feet deep.

"Here's what it's supposed to look like," I said to Mark, handing him the dimensions and showing him a picture of a raised bed from my library book.

Off he went to the local home improvement warehouse, where the knowledgeable staff set him up with railroad ties treated with magic chemicals to prevent rotting. What a good idea! He dug and leveled and stacked railroad ties and drilled and pounded long rebar poles deep into the earth to hold the whole thing together.

Soil was the next step, so I was thrilled when I saw a truck advertising "Topsoil" in the lane next to me at a traffic light. *Topsoil must mean the loamy dark stuff my books recommended for planting things,* I thought to myself. I jotted down the phone number that was hand-painted on the side of the truck and called it as soon as I got home. Mark and I were both at work when our delivery arrived. Let me rephrase that: Mark and I were both at work when the pile of bright-red dirt mixed with bottle caps and broken glass was dumped in our driveway. It didn't look like the pictures in my books, but who was I to second-guess the professionals?

My plant order had already arrived, so I was in a hurry to get the bed made up for my new wards. I excelled at making beds inside—my mother had been to nursing school and taught us to make perfectly creased and angled hospital corners when putting sheets on mattresses. I wanted to bring to my garden bed that same attention to detail. After a dozen trips with the wheelbarrow from the driveway to the planting area, I looked at the expanse of red dirt framed by the railroad ties and knew something wasn't right.

A call to the garden center confirmed that the "topsoil" I had just purchased was pure Virginia clay. "You need to amend the soil with organic matter," the garden center advisor said. The bottle caps and broken glass probably didn't count.

I rushed out and bought four forty-pound bags of leaf compost. By now it was late on a Sunday, and I had to finish the project before work the next day or the plants would sit in the carport for another week. Raindrops started to fall, then pour from the sky in sheets. Pulling up the hood of my raincoat, I went to work, first hauling the 160 pounds of compost from the car to the garden bed, then stabbing open each bag with my shovel.

"Work the amendments into the clay to improve your soil composition," my garden center guru had advised. By this point the clay was so wet that, had I had a big enough potter's wheel, I could have fashioned the world's largest terracotta urn. Instead, I plunged in with my gloved hands to mix the black compost into what had become the red sea of my garden bed. Within minutes, the gloves transformed into swamp monster paws. I tossed them aside and resorted to squishing handfuls of clay and leaf mold together with my bare hands, the doughy mess oozing between my fingers. Rain puddled in the bed around me, reflected in the weak beam of my flashlight.

Well past my bedtime, I finally gave up, leaving a streaky mess of red-and-black muck in my wake. As an afterthought, I retrieved the new plants from the carport, scooped out a few holes and shoved the tender sprouts into the drowning soil.

Years later, I learned that working soil when it's too wet doesn't improve the composition of said soil—it actually hurts it. And those treated railroad ties? They're toxic to the environment.

CHAPTER 3

The New Nanny

Quitting my job was never part of the plan.

A year or so before my parents' divorce, my mother reentered the workforce as an insurance agent. I was eleven. Within her social circle of doctors' wives, she was now the lone working girl. I was both proud of and embarrassed by this. My insecurity about my family being different from the Beaver Cleaver existences of my upper-middle-class friends—first with my mother going back to work, then the divorce, then my father's suicide all in less than three years—manifested itself in an indiscriminate disdain for stay-at-home mothers, who clearly led shallower lives than ours, and were therefore raising shallower children than me.

My mother's income paid the bills but didn't leave much of a margin for generous allowances. I had already tasted the empowerment that comes with a paycheck even before our family circumstances changed. In my case, empowerment was strawberry flavored.

The summer between fourth and fifth grades, about a year before my parents' divorce, I worked in the strawberry fields of southwest Washington State. It was the only summer job legally open to ten-year-olds (these days you need to be twelve), and my friend Robin and I signed up. Waiting for the bus to pick us up at 5:00 a.m. on the first day of our three-week stint, our flat chests encased in matching halter tops we had sewn ourselves out of triangles of calico and twisted cotton cording, Robin and I kept our heads down amid our mostly teenaged colleagues.

Strawberry plants are low to the ground, perfect work for child labor. We made our way up and down each row on our hands and knees, often in misty or gentle or insistent Pacific Northwest rain, twisting strawberries off their stems and dropping them into wooden produce flats holding a dozen or so pint-sized containers. When a flat was full, we'd carry it to a truck, where the farm staff would first weigh our delivery, then punch holes in a card we wore on a string around our necks to keep track of our total output. I think we were paid something like seven cents per pound. We could eat as many of the berries (unwashed and undoubtedly covered in pesticides) as we liked. The inverse relationship between how much I ate and how much I got paid was one of my first business lessons.

Our bare backs, we soon discovered, were perfect targets in the berry wars that erupted without warning from time to time. It would start with a single rotten berry hurled by a bored kid. The target and their buddies would retaliate, and before long whole handfuls of berries were being smashed between shoulder blades and on tops of heads until an overseer intervened. Not having bra straps with which to contend made berry war cleanup a little easier, but our hands were so stained from yanking hundreds of berries off their stems each day that we had to resort to bleach if we cared to clean them.

I made $200 that summer and bought a sewing machine. Earning my own money gave me a sense of independence and self-worth at a time when the rest of my life was unraveling and very much outside my control.

I looked for moneymaking opportunities wherever I could find them during my middle school and high school years. Both of my sisters had moved on to college, and my mother and I were on our own. If I wasn't babysitting, scooping ice cream, or mopping floors at the local Montessori school, I would play man of the house by chopping firewood, washing the car, hanging wallpaper, and even doing some minor electrical work. Mowing the lawn had always been women's work even when my dad was around, so it was a given that I'd take on the Toro duties both at home and for some of the neighbors.

One of my most lucrative entrepreneurial endeavors involved capitalizing on a freakish natural disaster in 1980—the eruption of Mount St. Helens. I was a sophomore in high school when the volcano blew its top. We lived in Vancouver, Washington, about sixty miles west of the mountain, and even though the winds streamed toward the east that day, several inches of powdery ash fell on our town. Ka-ching! Once the dust settled, I went door-to-door offering to hose off rooftops and unclog gutters. I wore a paper surgical mask to provide some semblance of protection from ash damage to my lungs. Fortunately, nobody asked whether I was licensed or insured.

My résumé lengthened further during college and graduate school, with numerous work-study jobs, research assistant positions, and temping gigs in offices. And although my master's degree came with a small mountain of student debt, I had gained a footing in a career that could pay it back. Simply put, I was wired to work.

When Mark and I bought the house, our budget was based on the assumption that I would always be working at least half-time. Not only did I enjoy working, I felt it was important for kids to see their mother going to the office and working alongside men. On an even deeper, unspoken level, earning my own paycheck was a safety net if the marriage were to fall apart. Keeping my own bank account solidified my sense of security and control.

Despite my fears that I wouldn't be able to conceive—I had spent the past decade trying *not* to get pregnant, and believed my body was now stuck in no-baby mode—our first son, Cody, arrived eighteen months after our wedding. My job's benefits package was based on European standards, which provided three months of paid maternity leave, unheard of in most American companies. Mark made a creative proposal to the federal agency he worked for that pieced together three months' worth of paid and unpaid leave. His customized paternity leave package was approved for months four to six of Cody's life, after which we'd both be comfortable leaving him with a nanny. Child care center hours were too confining for our schedules.

I spent most of my maternity leave staring in disbelief at my perfect baby. Whether it was because I was having my first child at the age of thirty-one, or because I was so frightened of wanting something as much as I wanted a baby, or because I was like every other pregnant mother who's ever walked the face of the earth, I had kept a running list in my head of everything that could go wrong while my baby cooked inside of me. The sonogram incited a little scream from me, since the image looked more like the creature that burst from John Hurt's stomach in *Alien* than the tender 3-D images that expectant parents coo over today. I had a recurring nightmare that our son would be born with Mikhail Gorbachev's birthmark covering his face. If I hadn't had my work to distract me, the delivery would have taken place in a padded cell.

Holding Cody in my arms, surrounded by piles of unfolded laundry (things went downhill quickly after my mother's two-week visit was up), I said to him, "If you are anything other than perfect from here on out, it will be my fault." How often I've looked back on that moment with nostalgia and guffawed at the notion that I could ever have that much power.

Mark would come home from work, kiss the baby and me, and say brightly, "What did you two do today?" Polite enough question, if I'd had anything to report. When I wasn't staring at the baby, all I did was breastfeed (which still entailed staring at the baby), pump milk to freeze for my return to work, change diapers, and wash clothes. I don't remember cooking. I don't remember cleaning the house. I don't remember even thinking those might be my responsibilities. I do remember yelling at Mark, "Stop asking me what I did all day!" He recalibrated quickly to, "How was your day?"

When my maternity leave was up, I felt more than ready to head back to the office. Knowing that Cody would be in Mark's care made the transition easier on the emotional side. The only glitch was that I had broken my ankle skiing about two weeks before I was scheduled to go back to work. With the cast, my briefcase, and the electric breast pump camouflaged as a stylish computer case swinging on my shoulder, I made a clunky reentry. Being back in the orderly environment of my office reinvigorated my sense of self. My to-do lists at work made sense to me and were fulfilling in a way that folding laundry could never be. My boss, a woman who had raised two children of her own while pursuing a demanding career, was thoroughly supportive. If my office door was closed, it was understood that I was either draining my udders or taking a ten-minute power nap to reboot my brain after a sleep-deprived night. If we had a deadline to meet, she would ask permission to come in while I was pumping. I'd take notes with my right hand while holding the pump to my breast with the left. Members of the old boys' club weren't invited.

I had looked forward to asking Mark innocently at the end of the day, "So, what did you two *do* today?" When I posed that question the evening of my first day back at work, he reported a list of accomplishments that far exceeded my three-month total. He had even completed the one non-baby-related task I was supposed to have taken care of during my three months at home—sell my beloved Toyota Starlet. I had purchased the car, a bank repossession, for $850 in cash to transport me from Seattle to Boston for graduate school. A baby's shoe was lodged under the front passenger seat when I took ownership. That little car (it even had a choke!) had not only moved me across the country, but had served as a moving storage unit and, on a couple of occasions, temporary housing when I was hunting for a job. A big shiny Jeep Grand Cherokee had taken the Starlet's spot in the driveway months earlier (Mark had lobbied for a minivan, but I would have none of that nonsense), relegating my Starlet to the street. I just couldn't bring myself to abandon my loyal old friend. Not so Mark—he unloaded it for $400 my first day back at work. I smiled tightly and congratulated him.

I told myself my husband was more productive because he had freedom of movement, whereas I had been attached quite literally to either a baby or a breast pump for a good portion of my maternity leave. I had secretly hoped that full-time child care would do him in, leading to a greater appreciation of why I had accomplished absolutely nothing during my own leave.

But when I arrived home from work each night, the table would be set, dinner was ready to be served up, and neat piles of washed and folded laundry were stacked on the coffee table if they hadn't been put away already. The ego boost I had absorbed at the office fizzled away.

Mark also had the weather in his favor, with his leave falling in May, June, and July. Since he was making everything look so easy, I upped the ante in the to-do lists I left for him. My little cutting garden had actually produced some flowers despite its soggy, misguided debut. The reemergence of the perennials planted a year earlier made my heart leap. Hungry for more, I asked Mark to create a new planting area off one end of the patio, a task that would include extending the bricked area to make room for a bench nestled between the flowers. I was getting used to having a combination husband/wife/handyman at my beck and call.

Although we had had some concern about what impact the unprecedented paternity leave would have on his career, Mark was offered an even better position to which to return. The internal staff memo announcing the appointment even noted that he was returning from paternity leave. In the annals of the Central Intelligence Agency (CIA)—did I mention that my husband worked at the CIA at the time?—it was a first.

Finding a nanny felt like a weeks-long root canal. We wanted someone to come to the house each day rather than a live-in. She had to be reliable enough to arrive on time, braving some of the worst traffic in the country. She had to be loving, motivated, smart, creative, patient, responsible, a fluent English speaker, and equipped with a medical degree, formal training in early childhood education, and a magic

Mary Poppins bag. Shannon hit about 75 percent of our wish list, leaps and bounds ahead of the competition.

As planned, Mark went back to work when Cody was six months old, and we settled into our new routine. I would come home from work, Shannon would show me the detailed list she had made of every feeding, every diaper changed, and every new or interesting feat my baby had accomplished that day. After she left, I would transfer my bottles of milk from the ice-packed section of my breast pump camouflaged as a computer bag. Then I would dance around the kitchen with Cody until he spit up on my suit.

We couldn't get enough of his smiles. The child woke up smiling and went to bed smiling. We'd keep him up late just so we could have more time with our happy baby, tickling him or bouncing him on our knees or singing loudly to him if his eyes started to droop, setting in motion sleep issues for the poor boy that continue almost two decades later.

Just after Cody's first birthday, when Shannon's daily "Here's What You Missed Today" lists (my title, not hers) were getting quite long, she sheepishly informed us that she had met a guy on the Internet and was moving to another state to be with him. She gave us her two-weeks' notice and skipped town. The prospect of looking for another nanny sent me into an existential crisis.

When Shannon started working for us, Cody was still a late sleeper. After my early morning feeding, he'd go back to sleep for several hours and I'd slip off to work. As the months progressed, he needed less sleep and would wake again before I left for work, drawing me in with his bright morning grin and wrenching my heart out when I had to leave. It became harder and harder to focus on the details of Slovenia's economic development (one of the sixty countries in my portfolio) when I was wondering if my son was taking his first steps. I considered telling Shannon to knock him over if he looked too steady on his feet, just so I could be there when he started walking.

On top of that, my cushy position in my no-travel job was coming to the end of its term limit. Any next step in my career would require several overseas trips a year, just as Cody was starting to talk, walk, and explore the world. Thoroughly demoralized after interviewing the first two prospective nannies sent from the agency, I burst into tears.

Mark didn't know what that noise was. It may have been the first time he had heard me cry. When I told him between sobs that I didn't want someone else taking care of my baby, he looked at me blankly for a minute then headed for the calculator. After running the numbers, he figured we could survive for a few months on his income alone, then I could find something part-time.

I called my mother. "I found a new nanny," I said. "She has the same name and birthday as I do."

"That's weird," she said. "What are the chances of that? When does she start?"

CHAPTER 4

Zigzag Mama

A minivan was never part of the plan. A minivan was on the same list as living in the suburbs, quitting my job, and washing smudges off my kid's face with my own spit.

But we had another baby on the way, our ninety-pound chocolate Labrador, Java, accompanied us on road trips in a bulky crate, and grandparents often joined us for excursions. Mark lobbied hard for a minivan despite my protestations that driving one would be the nail in the coffin of my self-respect.

"Just test-drive it," he persisted.

It wasn't the better gas mileage or more comfortable ride that sold me, both of which were far superior to the cooler SUV option, I had to admit. What turned the tide in the months-long minivan debate was that, once I actually opened up the back of one, I saw that a minivan could serve as the pickup truck I needed to support my gardening addiction.

By the time Jacob, our second son, was born, I had four seasons of gardening under my belt. I was just beginning to believe it wasn't an anomaly that the papery brown bulbs I planted in the fall actually emerged in broad strokes of color the following spring. The black-eyed Susans and hostas that Diane had passed over the fence to me during my earliest forays into the garden had not only survived my neglect (I doubt I had even watered them), but had somehow come back each year bigger and better than before. The spring after the hostas' first dormancy in my garden, the strange whirled tips poking through the earth gave me a bit of a fright: I had completely forgotten about them. Their reemergence chipped away at something deep within me. Trust had never been my strong suit, but those hostas seemed to say, "I'll be there for you no matter what."

I wanted to dip my brush into other types of plants and landscape designs, but there simply wasn't enough time between changing diapers, getting everyone fed, keeping clean clothes on their backs, and driving around to our myriad activities to make anything but slow progress in the garden. I would spy on Diane out of my second-story bathroom window as she perused her lush garden beds in her bathrobe on sunny mornings, a steaming cup of coffee in one hand, a pair of pruners in the other. Then the baby would cry and I'd be pulled back to reality.

At the height of planting season, I was making several runs to the garden center each week. The minivan allowed me to buckle two car seats into the middle row and load up several hundred pounds of mulch behind the kids. The cargo area accommodated several flats of plants, tall shrubs, and even small trees. If necessary, I could squeeze in plants and soil amendments and the dog, eventually sealing my cost-benefit analysis in favor of the minivan. But in those early days, my ego took a hit on two fronts, both because of the style-cramping nature of the beast and because I had so publicly insisted to family and friends that I would never, under any circumstances, succumb to the suburban mom-mobile. I was also regularly cleaning my kids' faces with my own spit.

Gardening filled the narrow spaces between the non-negotiables. I had moved almost immediately, and with great appreciation, to a new part-time job. After quitting my original higher-profile position, another department in the same organization offered me a half-time arrangement that allowed me to work mostly from home. Although economic policy analysis—the work for which I had been trained—wasn't part of the job, I wouldn't need to travel and could tailor my work time to avoid rush hour. By the time Jacob was born, I had switched to periodic contract projects that I could do entirely from home.

Work hours were squeezed in before the boys woke up, when they napped, and after we put them to bed at night. And although I had part-time childcare help from my mother-in-law, young Katy next door (who did, indeed, become the world's best babysitter), and a local childcare provider before preschool started, deadlines often materialized when I had the boys on my own at home.

I was scrambling to meet one of those deadlines when the boys were about two and four years old. Cody called upstairs, "Mommy, come see Jacob."

"Just a minute, I'm finishing up a report that somebody's waiting for me to send," I called down from my office upstairs.

"No really, Mommy, you need to come see Jacob."

"I just need about two more minutes here, sweetheart, then I'll be down," I promised.

"Mommy . . ."

"Just one more minute," I said, annoyance bubbling to the surface.

Java roused himself from where he'd been sleeping at my feet and lumbered downstairs to check things out, his toenails clicking on the hardwood stairs. He didn't come back.

Ten (fifteen?) minutes later, I sent off my report, replied to a few emails, and went downstairs to where I thought the boys were playing and watching *Bob the Builder*. Bob was there on the

TV screen, solving some problem in that quiet way of his (Bob was a man of few words), but his audience was nowhere to be seen. I heard giggling in the bathroom and my stomach turned. The door was ajar. With more than a little trepidation, I pushed it open to find Cody, arms spread wide in a triumphant "ta da!" pose, presenting my silky-skinned and fair-haired youngest. Jacob was standing in the toilet. Not *on* the toilet but *in* the toilet. Following his big brother's orders, Jacob had been waiting patiently for me all that time to come and see him. While he waited, toilet water had slowly soaked into every fiber of his fuzzy red one-piece footie pajamas, all the way up to his neck and all the way down to his wrists. When I stripped him out of the dripping casing, his feet were prune-like from marinating in toilet water.

I tried to keep them in sight from then on, fearing that Child Protective Services would show up any day to snatch my children away. But it was hard to stay focused on a business call when my sons were jousting with the fireplace tools.

Parenting resources piled up on my nightstand. I moved books like *The Making of United States International Economic Policy* and *Dollar Politics* to the basement to make room on my office shelves for *1-2-3 Magic: Effective Discipline for Children 2–12, How to Talk So Kids Will Listen and Listen So Kids Will Talk,* and *Siblings without Rivalry.*

Everything I read about child development suggested that more was better—more sensory experiences to spark new neural connections, more reading, more art projects, more social interaction, more stimulation of pretty much any kind short of illegal drugs. We racked up miles in the minivan driving to classes at the nearby farm, book readings at the library and the local bookstore, and visits to the zoo, children's museum, aquarium, or one of the many Smithsonian museums at our disposal in Washington, D.C.

There was never a shortage of activities to explore. Layered onto the educational experiences were toddler exercise classes at Gymboree, gymnastics classes when they were a little older and, once they'd celebrated their fifth birthdays, soccer. They quickly grew out of many of those early activities, but once soccer started, it never stopped. Ever.

Our calendar was always full, not only with kids' activities, but also with my own. I saw this as efficiency (economists are all about efficiency). If a square on my calendar was empty, I made sure to find something to fill it—another volunteer activity, another museum visit with the kids, another networking meeting for the day when I would be ready to take on more work. If my professional output was slipping away, I had to replace it with motherhood output, and, for a three-year period, granddaughter output as well. We had moved my father's mother, who suffered from increasingly severe dementia, to a nearby assisted-living facility. Managing my grandmother's care required frequent trips not only to visit her, take her shopping, and bring her home to see the boys, but also to transport her to the emergency room every few weeks for emphysema episodes and other crises (including a dog bite).

Our home environment whipped my stress levels to stiff peaks. I was too busy getting us organized for activities or working in the garden to worry about picking up the house. Books, papers, laundry, toys—it was the mess I'd let accumulate in my studio apartment days multiplied by a thousand. For whatever reason, I had never owned my own laundry hamper, at least not the grown-up kind that stands up by itself as opposed to a drawstring bag that takes way too long to put your clothes into every time you undress. Mark had a hamper—an ugly beige guy hamper with air holes in the sides—but my clothes didn't like to be confined there. It was Java who finally trained me to use the thing after eating about a dozen pairs of my dirty underwear. Mark did most of the dishes, so at least we didn't have mold growing in the sink (more fodder for Child Protective Services). A magnet on the refrigerator announced "A Clean House Is a Misspent Life."

The piles accumulated both in number and height as school forms and homework and artwork started to come home with the kids. Once they were old enough to notice that field trip permission slips needed to be filled out by a certain date and that there was no hope of finding the form in the tsunami that comprised my desktop, meltdowns on all our parts became an almost daily occurrence.

And then there was the testosterone. Having grown up with sisters, I was unprepared for the physicality of boys. They hit each other. They kicked each other. They bit each other. They tripped each other. They threw things at each other. Not just my boys, I came to learn. All boys. Or at least many boys. Or at least enough boys so that more than one person reassured me that my boys were normal. I wasn't so sure.

Even if they weren't actually trying to hurt each other, we still ended up in the emergency room multiple times as a result of their "just being boys." Stitched up chin, stitched up eyebrow, stapled head, glued head. If only the ER or urgent-care center had offered frequent-flier memberships.

When the kids were around seven and four, I went to a parenting class in search of guidance on how to stop their fighting. Their pummeling of one another lit a fuse in me that I was unable to extinguish. Screaming had become my first course of action, which often resulted in a sore throat that reminded me for hours (if not days) that I had lost control. I kept throat lozenges in my purse.

As I explained to the parenting instructor, my sons seemed to take great joy in watching Mommy blow her top. Once they were both in time-outs in their separate bedrooms as punishment for fighting. I was trying to get work done in my office when I heard the sound of spanking and cries of pain. I flew in a rage to the source of the commotion. Each was still alone on his own bed, but Cody was slapping his thigh and Jacob was crying out in pain as if he had been hit. "Gotcha!" they laughed when I burst onto the scene, red-faced and yelling.

The instructor listened to my story. I knew I was central to the problem, but I couldn't find a way out. She took a pencil and paper and  drew a picture of a stick figure woman. Then she drew zigzags all around the figure. She let me get a good look at the picture before continuing.

"This is you," the instructor said, stabbing the zigzag mama with her pencil. Moving the tip of her pencil to the jagged lines surrounding the figure, she continued, "This is the stress energy that you are emitting into your home. It's contagious."

Boom. Though I felt as though I had been kicked in the stomach, I knew she was right. The throat lozenges in my purse seemed to vibrate in agreement. I had been blaming the boys for misbehaving, taking it as a personal affront, but I realized at that moment that I was like a KitchenAid mixer, churning us all into a frothy mess of short-tempered reactivity. Though I'd had an epiphany, it would be years before I discovered the secret to dissolving those negative zigzags.

In the meantime, the garden was always in the background, beckoning from my kitchen window, catching my attention as I pulled out of the driveway. I wanted to be there. The garden was a source of calm I couldn't muster on my own. Only in the garden did my breathing slow, my heart rate settle, my mind quiet down. Like a mother stroking my hair, the garden soothed my inner hysteria. My pent-up stress energy powered my planting efforts: pulling up turf to create new beds, rebuilding the Virginia clay with bag after bag of soil amendments (I had started to compost, but my demand far exceeded my supply), digging up existing shrubs to move to another spot in the yard, planting a better shrub in the old shrub's place, digging up something to give to Diane next door in exchange for an import from her garden.

The garden babysat the boys while I weeded, planted, and pruned. She took them by the hand and led them to the wonders that lay beneath her soil, under her rocks, high in her branches, and amid her blooms. Earthworms and ladybugs and pollen-covered bumblebees brought squeals of delight and, as they got older, shouts of "Hey, look at this!" The discovery of a praying mantis would be so overwhelming that we could only express our astonishment in whispers.

We built stepping-stone paths through shrub tunnels only big enough for kid bodies to squeeze through. When a neighbor's massive tree came down, I rolled pieces of the trunk up the steep slope to create a stump table and a circle of stump chairs. My sons each had their own patch of garden space where, for a few years at least, they helped plant flowers they had chosen themselves from plant catalogs. Like Shel

BLOOMING INTO MINDFULNESS

Silverstein's *The Giving Tree,* the garden allowed them to dig and climb and build secret hideaways while never asking for a thing in return.

One balmy July evening, not long after the epiphany-producing parenting class, I sat on the front lawn watching the boys catch fireflies in the twilight. The air was comfortably humid and drenched with the aroma of freshly mown grass. Crickets warmed up for their nightly concert; the sky moved from faded to ever deeper shades of denim blue. Cody wore the Indian costume I had sewn for him for Halloween two years earlier, his seven-year-old wrists sticking several inches out of the sleeves, and the elastic waistband pants slung low on his hips. Wisps of brown hair escaped from his single-feathered headdress as he searched the shrubs, flower beds, and lawn for the twinkling lights that exposed his prey.

Four-year-old Jacob wore the Batman costume I had stitched together for him almost two years earlier. The stretchy velour fabric could still accommodate his growth, although the pants' hemline hit him mid-calf. With his black satin cape torn slightly at the neckline, he looked like a miniature Caped Crusader stranded on a desert island. He ran to me, blond hair shimmering in the encroaching darkness, and slowly unfurled his fingers to show me his prize. The firefly capitalized on the moment and escaped its sweaty trap. I held my breath and waited for Jacob's reaction. "That was fast!" he exclaimed, as the bug disappeared into the sky. He now had enough experience to know that, for patient hunters, the firefly supply was endless. He took off his cape and used it to cover his bug holder, a jar with a wire mesh top alight with blinking captives.

In the meantime, Cody had climbed a dogwood tree, his empty quiver catching on the branches behind his shoulder. He jumped into the night with a war cry and rolled like a stunt-man down the hill. Thrilled by the sensation, he climbed back up the tree and jumped over and over again. I was lulled by the sense of safety my children seemed to take for granted. Savoring this realization, I managed to take it in stride when Cody's Indian costume split down the back during an especially exuberant roll down the hill.

Unfortunately for all of us, the garden's soothing effect on my mind was confined to when I was in actual contact with the soil. Folding laundry, driving the minivan, browsing the aisles of the grocery store, cooking dinner, waiting for soccer practice to finish—through it all my head spun with thoughts about the future:

Where do you need to get the kids to next?

What are you going to do with them in the summer once school vacation starts?

How are you going to fit in more paid work when you're already crazy busy?

And even if you did have time, what kind of work do you even want to do anymore?

I wondered when my real life would begin again. I didn't regret my decision to change course and prioritize my family; I had even let go of my resistance to the minivan. But I saw this home-based stage as temporary, just one short chapter to slog through until the day when I wouldn't have to take care of everyone else. I enjoyed being with my kids and recognized fully the luxury of having that choice. But I was rarely fully present with them or able to accept them as they were in that moment. I kept waiting for them to grow up, to stop fighting, to help more around the house, to be old enough to understand my jokes. And why were they so offended by my sarcasm, anyway?

What would my next chapter look like and when would it start? And why weren't they noticing and acknowledging everything I had sacrificed to be there for them? That grumbling voice echoed in my head again and again.

Resentment crept into every fiber of my being, like the toilet water in Jacob's fuzzy footie pajamas.

CHAPTER 5

Master Gardener

A nother master's degree was never part of the plan. Although the minivan had grown on me (and perhaps even because of this), my fear of losing my professional identity only deepened. My existential crisis generated an inner turmoil that bubbled over into my interactions with Mark, the kids, and the rest of the world. I avoided gatherings where someone might ask me, "What do you do?" Before I had children, I had always had some sort of respectable reply to that question, whether it was a specific job or an academic endeavor. But although I had set up shop as an independent contractor with full legal standing as a privately held company, I was taking on only two or three paid projects a year, sometimes even fewer. I didn't want to work more. I wanted to garden more. But, just as I didn't believe at the time that "I'm a mom" was enough of a reply to the "What do you do?" question, that was even more true for "I'm a gardener."

Recognizing my ego's need for a labeled credential, Mark signed me up for the Fairfax County Master Gardeners program as a surprise birthday gift when I turned thirty-five. I knew nothing about the three-year certification program, which is not a university master's degree, but a combination of training and volunteerism to support the Virginia Cooperative Extension's outreach programs. After a year on the waitlist, I entered the program in 2000.

Cody was four and Jacob was one-and-a-half years old during my first year. I was exhausted by the time Mark got home from work to take over caring for the kids so that I could make it to the night classes. After plastering the dark circles under my eyes with a thick layer of concealer and running a brush through my greasy hair, I kissed everyone goodbye and closed the door on dirty dishes, half-eaten meals, and crying kids. I didn't mind the rush-hour traffic; my time alone in the car was as luxurious as a spa treatment.

Some nights it was hard to stay awake during class (especially if we were talking about turf), but most classes were riveting. Until then, I had thought about plants primarily in terms of flower color. In class, I learned that different plants required different climates and soil types, and had different water and light needs. Color, in fact, was probably the least important factor to consider when choosing a plant for a particular site.

The Virginia Cooperative Extension agent—one of many speakers who taught the Master Gardeners curriculum—pounded away on the importance of learning plants' botanical names. *Is she kidding?* I thought to myself. *If I wanted to work that hard, I would have gone back to college.* Chasing two little boys around all day left me little energy for hard thinking after about 10:00 a.m., let alone after sundown. Whether due to fatigue, data overload in my hard drive, or aging, my brain was no longer the pliable machine that had processed new vocabulary relatively easily in my youth. A stubborn fight ensued when I asked it to memorize foreign botanical names and their translations.

Entomology was another challenge. Diagnosing plant problems, it turns out, requires knowing about different insects' mouth parts, specifically whether the little bugger was designed for sucking, chewing, piercing, or sponging. Those different mouths leave different signs and symptoms on plants, essential clues when determining a plan of action. I had abandoned the sciences years earlier, and cobwebs mucked up whatever part of my brain was responsible for identifying and remembering insect anatomy. But how could I not be fascinated to learn that there are more species of insects than of any other taxonomic group, making up half of all global species? Who knew? I couldn't wait to tell the boys that sucking bugs inject salivary enzymes into their food (whether plants or another insect) to liquefy the tissue before sucking it up through their styla, or food-sucking tube. Most importantly, learning some science made me feel as if there was some heft to my Master Gardener status. If need be, I could even sprinkle a few science facts into dinner party conversation if I was feeling insecure about my stay-at-home mom status.

The entomology training didn't scare me, but the class on invasive plants gave me goosebumps. There seemed to be no limit to evil forces in our midst.

My fear of invasives started with the snakehead. In 2002, a rapidly growing population of the snakehead *(Channidae)* fish was discovered in a pond in Maryland, not far from where I live. Its looks alone gave the fish a bad rap, in particular its protruding lower jaw and big mouth filled with long, sharp, shiny teeth. It all started when a man in Crofton, Maryland, ordered two live snakeheads from an Asian fish market in New York. Snakeheads had been prized in his native Hong Kong for their curative properties, and he intended to cook them into a soup for his ailing sister. (I guess it's the Asian version of my Jewish mother-in-law's chicken soup.) But by the time the fish arrived, his sister had recovered. He kept the snakeheads in an aquarium for a while, but they were ravenous little beasts and required more and more goldfish to fill their bellies, eventually wearing out their welcome. So he dumped them into a nearby pond.

The problem was that snakeheads have no natural enemies in the United States. They can thrive in a wide range of temperatures and can live in muddy or plant-filled ponds, swamps, or streams. Creepiest of all is that snakeheads can breathe air and survive for up to four days out of water, and even longer if they've burrowed into the mud. They can travel over land, slithering from one body of water to another, a talent that served them well during the dry season in their native habitats in Asia and Africa. Snakeheads have been described as "voracious eaters that prey on fish, crustaceans, frogs, insects, small reptiles, birds, and mammals, with significant impacts on food chains and ecosystems. Adults may attack humans who approach young."[1] It's not surprising that movies were made about snakehead invasions, including *Night of the Snakehead, Swarm of the Snakehead,* and *Snakehead Terror.* The snakehead infestation was discovered in that Maryland pond a few months after the 9/11 terrorist attacks. The Pentagon is just a few metro stops from my town. The year of the snakehead, 2002, was also the year of the Beltway sniper attacks, during which two gunmen shot victims randomly in the Washington, D.C., metropolitan area, including the Maryland and Virginia suburbs, killing ten people and wounding three others. Those of us living in the danger zone spent three weeks ducking behind our cars while filling our tanks at gas stations in case the snipers had us in their viewfinders. I remember running in zigzag patterns from the car through the parking lot into the grocery store, making a game of it with the boys while hiding the fact that I was actually keeping our movements unpredictable and hard to target.

When I learned in my Master Gardeners class that I also needed to worry about invasive plants, it just about put me over the edge. The title alone of the handout we received, "Invasive Alien Plant Species in Virginia," made me want to dig a bunker and move underground long before planning for the zombie apocalypse became fashionable.

According to the Department of Conservation and Recreation and the Virginia Native Plant Society, invasive alien plant species typically exhibit the following characteristics:

rapid growth and maturity; prolific seed production; highly successful seed dispersal, germination and colonization; rampant vegetative spread; ability to outcompete native species; and high cost to remove and control.[2]

Sounds a lot like the snakehead.

So many things are out of our control when we garden—the weather, the seventeen-year cicada cycle, a bird pooping the seed of an alien plant into your backyard. Gardeners look for empowerment wherever they can find it. For me, it was pruning.

Diane had already taught me the power of pruning before I started my Master Gardeners classes. I had watched her cut back five-foot-tall azaleas to stubs measuring a foot or less from the ground. When I saw that hers grew back not only quickly but more vibrant than before, I mustered the courage to try pruning some of my own, with the same positive results. The techniques I learned in my classes emboldened me to take my pruners to other plants. Though I was skeptical, it turned out to be true that cutting perennials back during their early growth period encourages more stem growth, which in turn produces more blooms.

I went through an Edward Scissorhands phase, during which I clipped, lopped, and sawed anything within reach to put my mark on it. The more I touched the plants, the more

I thought of them as "mine." The whole garden, in fact, was "mine," and the boys could play in it as long as they didn't hurt "my" plants. They had been trained at an early age to not pull up my plantings, although telling them to watch where they stepped during a game of tag or hide-and-seek was fruitless. Even the garden's calming influence couldn't always stop me from barking at them.

Speaking of barking, I had to start that training all over again when we got a new puppy in the fall of 2001. Earlier that year, our beloved Java lost a run-in with a car after escaping from the house. Although I had wanted to wait at least a year before getting another dog (Ahhh—to have a dog mess-free back lawn!), I knew we needed a distraction when I found myself debating with three-year-old Jacob the correct pronunciation of Osama bin Laden. ("No Mommy, it's Sambaladen!")

What better way to take your kids' minds off a terrorist attack than to bring home a puppy? I surprised them with an eight-week-old yellow Labrador/Golden Retriever mix chosen from a litter in the Virginia countryside. We named him Spirit. Jacob had suggested Ghost because of the puppy's white coat, which was a stronger argument than Cody could produce with his suggestion of Dolphin. Spirit, another version of Ghost, symbolized the lifting of our spirits that came with our squirmy bundle of puppy. It wasn't long before our spirited Spirit was stealing my gardening gloves to force a chase around the yard and pulling up my plants by their roots.

Later the name would take on much deeper significance for me. In the meantime, Spirit's wild, uncontrollable puppy energy, combined with the similar energy of his two-legged brothers, bumped my stress levels to new heights. None of them showed any respect for my Master Gardener status or any other credential. My negative zigzag energy intensified.

CHAPTER **6**

Poisoned

Poisoning plants was never part of the plan.

By 1998, our fourth year in the house, I had filled my sunny planting areas in the railroad-tie cutting garden and the half-moon bed that Mark had built off the side of the brick patio. My next obsession became transforming the plateau along the top of the back slope. I wanted to look out my kitchen window and see a gardener's landscape, not the eighty feet of naked wooden fence line that stretched the width of the property.

I awoke thinking about that planting bed. I went to sleep thinking about that planting bed. And in between, if I wasn't pacing back and forth along the expanse of the fence line pondering what to put there, I was in my kitchen staring out the window at the planting bed.

Why was it so important to me? Part of it had to with that voice in my head that demanded I have a label. If I was

62

no longer a working economist, I had to at least be a credible gardener in the eyes of the world. The view from my kitchen window would validate me.

It was about more than the label, though. Planting, I had come to learn, provided instant gratification in a way that my former career never could. My professional work had lost its appeal because I was geographically far removed from whatever impact I might have had. I needed to see and feel the results of my labor. Growing plants—and, even more so, growing boys—was exponentially more satisfying, though I still resisted this emerging realization. Even more importantly, on the days when I couldn't see positive change anywhere else in my life, I could stick a plant in the ground and feel I had made a difference in the world.

A tug-of-war ensued in the garden between my parenting and my planting. A plastic Little Tikes log cabin took up real estate under the shady canopy of the honeysuckle on the right side of the back hilltop. The left side of the plateau was broader and flatter, but not by much. We thought about putting a swing set there, but the topography would require the swings to be perched on the edge of the slope. I had visions of kids jumping off at the height of an upswing and yelling, "I can fly!" before crashing through the dining room window—if the cherry tree didn't stop them first.

I could, however, create a fairly deep planting bed in front of the fence while still saving a strip of grass to kick a soccer ball a few feet before it rolled down the hill. The other honeysuckle tree, about twenty-five feet from the left corner, shaded a portion of the planting area, but I used that space to experiment with shade-loving plants, including ferns, hostas, and several clumps of lily of the valley that Diane had donated from her yard.

I drew a rough picture of the fence and the dimensions of the planting area, then headed to the garden center in search of recommendations. Along with my scribbled picture, I had a folder filled with pages ripped from gardening magazines showing lush, layered mixed borders with multi-seasonal interest. *All I need to do is copy this,* I told myself.

The garden center staffer looked at my drawing and my folder of photographs and said, "You really need a designer to put together a plan for something this extensive."

"I don't have time for a designer," I said. I was very pregnant with Jacob at the time and needed to get the plants in the ground before my due date in August. "Just make your best guess for a few recommendations to get me started. I'm in a bit of a hurry here."

Budget constraints and pregnancy forced me to prioritize. I couldn't afford to buy all the plants at once, nor would

I have enough time or energy to settle them into their new home before Jacob's arrival, so we started with woody plants to provide some structure in the back of the border.

I came home with *Enkianthus campanulatus* (redvein enkianthus), which was supposed to grow to be ten feet tall and serve as the anchor for the left corner. The garden center's shrub expert also recommended *Kolkwitzia amabilis* (beauty bush), a fountain-shaped woody shrub that blankets itself in pale pink flowers in the spring. A *Rhododendron* (rhododendron) and a *Buddleia* (butterfly bush) exhausted my budget that day.

Buddleia have a bad reputation for being invasive, but I hadn't yet started the Master Gardeners program, so ignorance was bliss. At the time I was planting as many butterfly attractors as I could. The home and garden magazines said that no self-respecting butterfly garden would be without a *Buddleia*. What I didn't know then was that dozens, if not hundreds, of other pollinator attracting plants are on the market that outshine the unkempt *Buddleia* in the looks department and, more importantly, are not on the invasives list. But at the time, discovering the magic of a butterfly convention converging on that gangly shrub made my heart flutter.

Over the next couple of years, the *Kolkwitzia* and *Buddleia* did fine, but the *Enkianthus* in the left corner floundered, never quite thriving. The ever-thirsty *Rhododendron* (whose water demands I didn't understand when I bought it out of nostalgia for the Pacific Northwest) died a slow death, stuck in the right corner of the hilltop too close to competing tree roots, not to mention being forced to suffer through Virginia's heat and humidity when all it really wanted was a cool and misty pocket of an Oregon forest to sink its roots into. Burying two cats in that same corner might have also had something to do with the plant's demise, whether through root disturbance or dead kitty juju.

But it was the left corner of the hilltop that was my real focus. Besides the *Kolkwitzia* and the *Buddleia* (the latter of which grew into a leggy unsightly mess that even butterflies couldn't transform), nothing else flourished there. I kept throwing more plants into the ground—too many to remember—and watched helplessly as they eventually yellowed, wilted, and died. Remembering the flush of instant gratification I had felt each time I sank a plant (and money) into that corner, I felt hoodwinked.

Shortly after Jacob was born, I asked an arborist to come and assess the health of our trees. Pointing to the barren back left corner, I said, "I'd really like to fill that area with plantings, maybe even another small flowering tree, but nothing seems to do well here."

"It's too bad you have a black walnut there," he said.

"I don't have a black walnut there," I protested.

"Yes, you do," he replied, pointing up. "It's right there."

"But that's on the other side of the fence."

Embarrassed for me, he said, "That's true, but the roots are on your property and the nuts and leaves fall inside your fence."

So that's what those big green balls were that I was constantly turning my ankle on.

"What's the big deal about black walnuts?" I asked.

"Have you heard of juglone?"

"No." The guy's patronizing tone was getting on my nerves.

It turns out that black walnut trees—in particular the roots but also decaying leaves and nuts—secrete a substance called hydrojuglone, which oxidizes into a toxic chemical named juglone. It's a survival mechanism to reduce competition, kind of like sneaking arsenic into other racers' drinks before a marathon. Lots of plants are susceptible to juglone poisoning. Lots and lots and lots of plants, many of which I had already planted in that area and watched as they withered away. All this time I had just thought it was something I was doing wrong—not enough water, too much water, not enough soil amendment, not the right type of mulch, dog peeing on the plants, kids stepping on them. All along, it had been the juglone.

I felt violated and angry at the black walnut. I thought about cutting it down, but it wasn't on my property. And anyway, the toxin-producing roots were too extensive to remove. This was war.

In my second year of the Master Gardeners program, the herbaceous plants class was taught by a woman who owned a plant farm in Aldie, Virginia, about twenty-five miles west of Vienna. Karen's deep horticultural knowledge and experience in growing unique cultivars convinced me that she would be a good advisor in my battle against juglone. I asked her to recommend some plants for my back fence area, including what I had come to think of as the black walnut's skull and crossbones corner.

Besides supporting my own gardening needs, a plant farm would be a perfect field trip for the boys (five and three years old at the time). The bonus was that they'd be strapped into their car seats for forty minutes each way, a total of eighty whole minutes of worry-free time with my sons. The click of the safety straps across their chests was like a little dose of Valium.

I pulled into the farm's gravel parking lot and gave my sons the usual lecture about not grabbing or knocking anything over. That included plants and each other. Freed from their constraints, they jumped out of the van and disappeared. We were the only customers there at the time, so it seemed safe to let them roam while I checked out the plants.

Karen waved to me from the edge of the nearest field and jogged over to the parking lot. "I have your recommendations ready," she said. "Let me just grab them from the office."

Other than a couple of plants I had flagged from the slideshow she'd presented in class, I didn't recognize most of the names on the list she produced a few minutes later: *Penstemon digitalis, Fothergilla gardenii, Aurinia saxatilis, Sedum sieboldii, Hakonechloa macra, Cimicifuga, Thalictrum aquilegifolium.*

Most of the plants were displayed on long tables inside weather-adjustable greenhouses that were designed like giant row covers. A light-filtering ceiling arched overhead and the walls extended down but stopped about three feet from the ground. The combination of dappled light and a gentle breeze seeping under the partial walls made me want to linger and contemplate each and every shade of green, each and every leaf form.

I could hear the boys playing in the greenhouse next to mine. They couldn't have been more than ten yards away, so I wasn't worried. I had learned by then that silence can be more dangerous than noise when it comes to little boys entertaining themselves, so their laughter and chattering next door was comforting.

It's good for them to be able to explore on their own, without me micromanaging all the time, I thought to myself. *It's good for them to discover the world together and have their own adventures.* I fell deeper into my plant-induced reverie.

Squealing pulled me out of my trance. Was that squealing laughter? Or squealing something else? I was lost in the intricacies of a *Thalictrum* blossom. More squeals of unbounded excitement. Hmmm . . . better take a look. I leaned down to look under the walls, but the ground-level view was blocked by five- and ten-gallon black plastic tubs of plants.

I left my greenhouse, walked a few paces, and entered the greenhouse where the boys were.

My sons were about fifteen yards from the door. Each was fixated on the same something, though Cody stood four or five feet behind Jacob.

"Hi guys," I said. "What's so interest . . ." I swallowed the rest of the word.

Jacob, his blond head glowing in the filtered light, stood stock still. Inches from his face, a huge black snake hovered eye-to-eye with my three-year-old. It must have been more than five feet long, enough to coil and rise to Jacob's full height. Like Kaa in *The Jungle Book,* the snake stared into my Mowgli's eyes with a hypnotic power that rendered all of us speechless.

Don't panic, I ordered myself. *One wrong move and the kid gets it.*

"Okay," I said quietly, "now—everybody stay very, very still." I tiptoed toward the boys. "Cody, back up very slowly, without moving your arms." Anything that disturbed the air-flow could trigger the snake to strike.

I leaned over, slid my hands under Jacob's armpits, and engaged every core muscle at my disposal to lift him gently up and away from the snake. We walked very slowly at first, then ran the rest of the way to the parking lot.

Once out of harm's way, the boys fell into excited giggles.

"Oh my god! What happened?" I asked.

"We thought it was a hose, but then it moved some," Cody said. "So then I told Jacob to throw some rocks at it."

Jacob nodded in agreement, happy to have played such an important role in the thrilling experiment.

I strapped them into their car seats (click!) and went to find Karen. "There's a giant snake in there!" I said breathlessly, pointing to the spot from which I had just rescued the boys. "It almost bit my son!"

"Oh, that's just Wilma," Karen said calmly. "She lives in there. She's a black rat snake—not poisonous—but she's blind and might have bitten if she was scared. Would have hurt like hell."

I had visions of the snake biting Jacob in the face, maybe even taking an eye out, which might have led to a severe case of not only ophidiophobia (a fear of snakes) on both our parts, but also agoraphobia, trapped inside for the rest of our lives out of fear of what might await us outside our doorstep. Maybe we'd become hermits, stop cutting our hair and fingernails, and take on other Howard Hughes habits, maybe . . . *snap out of it, Martha!*

I bought my plants, signing the credit card receipt with shaking hands, and hightailed it back to the suburbs, the image of my baby boy in a staring contest with a blind snake named Wilma seared into my memory.

Back at home, I released the boys into their natural habitat and filled my wheelbarrow with the plants I'd purchased from  Karen. As I pushed the load up the back hill, Wilma the snake was on my mind. How could I blame her? She had simply been lying in her regular spot soaking in the warmth of her jungle. I would have reacted in the same way if rocks were being thrown at me in the comfort of my own home. The boys got off easy. Wilma had had plenty of opportunity to bite, but she chose to gamble for a good long warning. She had more self-control than most of us.

Years later I would learn some of Wilma's skills. All of us have rocks thrown at us from time to time when we're just minding our own business. How do we react in those situations? When faced with a perceived threat, the ability to resist biting back goes a long way in diffusing a crisis. Paying very close attention to the source of negative energy—calmly staring it in the face like Wilma did—often dissolves it.

The black walnut tree was also just minding its own business when I came along and started to poke and prod at its roots. It was there first, long before our housing development was built. Who knew what it had seen? Civil War soldiers might have harvested those walnuts. Maybe native Americans had done the same. The tree's survival mechanisms had served it well. I planted my new batch of plants, did my best to keep the nuts and branches picked up, and hoped for the best.

More than a decade later, I learned in a *New Yorker* article by Michael Pollan (titled "The Intelligent Plant") just how astounding plants' survival mechanisms really are: "Many of the most impressive capabilities of plants can be traced to their unique existential predicament as beings rooted to the ground and therefore unable to pick up and move when they need something or when conditions turn unfavorable." He continues, "A highly developed sensory apparatus is required to locate food and identify threats. Plants have evolved between fifteen and twenty distinct senses, including analogues of our five: smell and taste (they sense and respond to chemicals in the air or on their bodies); sight (they react differently to various wavelengths of light as well as to shadow); touch (a vine or a root 'knows' when it encounters a solid object); and, it has been discovered, sound."[3]

If that doesn't deserve some respect, I don't know what does.

CHAPTER 7

The Escape

A bandoning the garden was never part of the plan. By the end of our first decade in the house, the garden had rewarded me for staying put. I had created wide new beds with sweeping curves around the entire backyard's fence line, the carefully chosen shrubs and perennials were—with the exception of the black walnut corner—flourishing, and lush plantings in hues of purple, chartreuse, and pops of pink and orange around a new flagstone patio flashed the message "A Gardener Lives Here."

We had even carved out a little vegetable garden in the strip of lawn next to our carport. I had enough work on my hands with the rest of the garden, so when Mark said, "When are we going to grow something we can eat?" I replied, "Whenever you feel like building a vegetable garden. And tending it, by the way."

In the process of building his second raised bed for the edibles, Mark managed to hammer a piece of rebar right through the inch-wide gas pipe buried two feet in the ground, a feat he was unlikely to have accomplished had he been trying. My announcement of "I smell gas" translated quickly into two shiny, red fire trucks showing up within minutes, a team of firefighters pointing a hose at Mark's work site, and a small crowd of interested neighbors on the sidewalk. The excitement ended when the hole was patched within a few minutes of the gas company's arrival.

Although I had hoped that Mark would become the edibles gardener in the family (a true gardening Gardiner), passions are not assignable. After a couple of years of vegetable garden duty—soil prep, crop planning, shopping, planting, weeding, and harvesting—it was clear that the spark never really ignited.

Mark made a valiant effort and produced some credible cucumbers, tomatoes, and green beans, but he just didn't feel the same pull to the garden that I did. His passion was soccer, and since five knee surgeries during his high school and college soccer careers had taken him out of the game, he got his fix by coaching both boys' teams and heading up the local youth soccer club's recreational program, which served more than two thousand kids. While vegetable gardeners were spending their weekend mornings picking slugs and hornworms off their tomato plants, Mark was driving to half a dozen soccer fields, either coaching or checking grass and turf conditions. I finally had to accept the fact that vegetable gardening just wasn't his thing.

The not fully untended but certainly undertended vegetable garden triggered my resentment about soccer taking over our lives, which, in turn, prompted an even deeper resentment about "my life" being put on hold. Though I didn't miss my office job, my self-worth was still tied to making money. No matter how grateful I was to be able to be home with my kids, my ego kept insisting this wasn't enough. I had grown to be unhappy in my paid job, but I still wasn't fully content being at home. It was still me vs. them. "My life" couldn't start until their lives (food, clothes, and sports) didn't absorb all of my time.

Soccer was the easiest scapegoat. Mark was also serving as our neighborhood association president at the time, in addition to traveling quite a bit for work. I'm the first to admit that these were first world problems for a wife, but they still intensified my first world stress and increased my output of negative zigzag energy.

My ego kept whispering, *You could be doing so much more with your life if you weren't stuck here doing everybody's laundry. Are you going to stoop even further and do Mark's vegetable gardening for him too?* I would have ignored the vegetable bed completely if it hadn't been located right next to the carport. Each time I headed to my car, I could swear I heard cries from the edibles of "We're here! We're here! We're HERE! Is anybody out there?"

"La la la la la," I sang out loud, my fingers stuffed into my ears until I was inside the car with the door closed. I gunned the engine and sped out of the driveway.

I had always assumed that my official "next chapter" would begin as soon as both kids were in school, when I would presumably be able to take on more work hours and perhaps even head back to some sort of office job to escape the chaos of my house. We had entered the twenty-first century by now, when it would surely be easy for women to work while their kids were in school. So why didn't our local elementary school start until 9:15 a.m.? And why was kindergarten still a half-day proposition at our public school? And why were all Mondays in our district half days for K–6?[4]

Our elementary school, excellent in every other respect, didn't have an after-care program, which meant that I'd have to hire another nanny or claw my way into daycare if I wanted to work from nine to five. A Brazilian bikini wax sounded more appealing than finding child care. The truth was, I liked being there when my kids got home from school, when they were most likely to talk about what had happened that day and I could get the best read on how they were dealing with life's curveballs.

To shut my ego up, I volunteered at the school, with Master Gardeners, and in the community. More and more volunteer hours crept into my schedule until there was no breathing room left. Nobody told me I could say no. Even if they had, my ego would never have allowed it. And when I wasn't volunteering, I was driving. And driving and driving and driving. Soccer practices, swim practices, gymnastics classes, all of it during rush hour on northern Virginia's notoriously congested roadways.

Weekends were devoted to soccer, which in the early days was relaxing and fun. Young families would settle themselves on blankets and chat, complimenting each other's munchkins as they followed the ball around the field like a swarm of bees. Families took turns bringing sliced oranges and juice boxes for the players. Snacks were shared with younger siblings. Butterflies fluttered along the sidelines, drawn to the communal sense of happy playtime.

Travel soccer started at age nine, though, and the butterflies bolted the field. Once real competition was introduced, some of the parents transformed into raving lunatics during games, screaming not only at referees, but at the tiny players themselves. I had to listen to sideline muttering about not enough playing time, questionable substitution choices, and other critiques of the coaches (aka my husband). I would not have been in that position if Mark had been a vegetable gardener instead of a soccer coach. It was all about me, after all. Most of the parents calmed down after the first couple of seasons, but I wouldn't have that perspective until years later.

Weather and daylight permitting, I would retreat to the garden after soccer games. Her quiet acceptance brought my heart rate down. Somewhere along the way I had started to think of the garden as a "she" instead of an "it," perhaps since she was such a strong antidote to the ocean of male energy in which I swam all the time.

One day I slipped a new hellebore out of its black quart-sized container. The plant seemed to be fine above the soil level, but its roots were choked inside their plastic confinement, swirled so tightly around the root ball that my fingers weren't strong enough to loosen them. I took my clippers and slashed the sides of the thick mass, sensing an "Ahhh—thank you!" from the plant as I loosened the noose and reopened its airways before burying it in its loamy new home.

I realized that I was as root-bound as that plant, squeezed in every aspect of my life. In the garden I had run out of room for more beds, and although I hadn't filled all my planting space, I felt guilty spending so much money on new plants when my income was so measly. Squeezed for time, I couldn't make more money. I knew I didn't really want to work outside the home but was nowhere close to being at peace with that decision, which squeezed my sense of self. Disgust over my internal whining took up whatever space remained in my head. I recognized what a luxury it was to have a partner who could support us all, even if my plant budget didn't go as far as I would have liked. I felt silly and petty, spoiled and grumpy, with no intention of letting go of any of it.

An opportunity for escape presented itself in 2005, when Mark was offered a posting in Stuttgart, Germany. The timing was perfect. The combination of our oxygen-sucking pace of life, my identity crisis, and the realization that I had lived in the same house for eleven years—longer by far than any other address my formerly nomadic self had ever occupied—stirred up a deep longing in me for a very, very long road trip. The prospect of boarding a plane for Europe and not coming back for three years felt like a lifeboat falling from the heavens. The kids were the perfect ages for it: Cody was nine and Jacob was six, old enough to remember the experience but young enough to not put up much of a fight about leaving their friends.

Long before we had final confirmation that Mark had gotten the job, I shifted into moving mode, drawing from the lessons my mother had taught me almost four decades earlier: start making lists and cleaning closets, and schedule a garage sale.

I dove in, praying that the final approval signatures for the posting would come through. My "Initial To-Do List for Germany Prep" included weeding out eleven closets, five rooms' worth of cupboards, drawers, and bookcases, three bathroom vanities, countless CDs and videos, kitchen cabinets and the pantry, laundry room shelves, one basement, two storage rooms, and the carport.

To attract renters to the house, we would need to fix some things: the wallpaper in the kitchen and laundry room was outdated; a hole gaped in the family room wall where a 1970s intercom system had been removed; the tub in the master bathroom was disintegrating and required reglazing; and both the foyer and the living room needed fresh paint.

Meanwhile, Mark was either working long hours, traveling, or trying to keep up with his volunteer commitments. We were both treading as fast as we could to keep our heads above water. But something about the process invigorated me even while it exhausted me. Why hadn't we taken that awful wallpaper down sooner? Why had we lived with the hole in the wall for so long? The fixes, though minor, were like a happy pill. But I wasn't quite sure why.

I was in full purge mode, relishing the process of shedding, clearing out, paring down. Why did we need all this stuff? Did our possessions constitute who we were? I didn't think so, especially since my whole notion of who I was had been turned on its head. Between the weight limit on what we could bring with us and the smaller house we would have on the military base where Mark's job was located, I felt I had a strong argument for getting rid of as much as possible.

Mark, on the other hand, just wanted to store everything. "Why do we need to get rid of any books?" he asked.

"Because we have two hundred books for toddlers and our kids are six and nine years old," I retorted. He took *Games to Play with Toddlers and Preschoolers* out of my "get rid of" pile and moved it to the "long-term storage" pile. I snatched it back and returned it to the "get rid of" pile. Things came to a head when he said he wanted to take the Harry Truman biography, which weighs about ten pounds, to Germany, even though we had both read it. When I asked why, he said, "Maybe we'll want to lend it to somebody."

And so it went. Not just with books, but with old clothes, coffee mugs from high school reunions, and broken candlestick holders. Getting him to let go of things was like pulling out impacted wisdom teeth.

The difference between us was that I felt weighed down by the bulk of our possessions. I still remembered clearly the days when I could fit most of what I owned into my Toyota Starlet. I could pick up and change course at a moment's notice—take flight on a whim. Fewer things represented freedom. For Mark, our possessions represented stability, nostalgia, comfort, and safety. Why go without when we had room to keep something? Another first world marital problem that required compromise.

The garden needed attention as well, but at least I was free to make my own choices there without argument from anyone. We knew that Mark was likely to get the job before the spring planting season began. Normally I would add a few unusual specimens to my plant collection when the weather warmed, but not this year. I couldn't leave vulnerable babies in the hands of utter strangers. So I went with safe bets that I wouldn't miss terribly if they perished in my absence. As for the established plantings, all I could do was cross my fingers and hope for the best.

I weeded, edged, and mulched every garden bed between school drop-offs and pickups. That is, unless I was doing laundry, grocery shopping, cleaning out closets and drawers, taking refresher German classes, or getting everyone to doctor's appointments to secure our medical clearances. Organizing garage sales and donation pickups, finding a property manager (and then a second one when the first one fell through), and every other task that goes into a move needed to be squeezed in between soccer and swim team commitments. My brief gardening sessions were a touchpoint for me, grounding and reassuring me along the way. The plants seemed to whisper, "Don't worry about us, we'll be fine!"

There were moments during moving preparations that brought me to my knees. When I was packing my office, I discovered in a crumbling stationery box two pages torn from a discarded autograph book from my childhood. How that thin, thirty-year-old Hallmark box had managed to escape my many purges over the years was beyond me. The square autograph-book pages, about four inches tall, contained messages in my father's neat handwriting.

"Keep smiling through good times and bad, and you will end up with the 'Golden Ring' of life. Stay happy and healthy. Love, Dad." It was dated July 5, 1974. And "May your future be filled with joy, happiness, and meaning—as you are capable of giving these feelings to others," from a message he wrote on February 18, 1975, about two years before his death. I knelt on the floor and wept while the boys chased each other through the house and Mark cleaned out the carport shed.

Somehow, we made it. Despite the fact that it had been close to twenty years since I had studied and worked in Germany, my German grammar bubbled up to the surface pretty quickly once we arrived, with vocabulary following on its heels.

We enrolled the boys in the international school, having made the calculation that had we placed them for three years in a German school, with at least a year spent learning the language, they might not be well-positioned academically once we were back home. Their language immersion took place on the soccer pitch while playing for the nearby village's club, and my American sons became quite proficient at swearing in German.

It was the first time in my adult life that I was completely without paid work, and the first time I was in an environment where nobody asked me what I "did." Once we had settled into our routine, I found my volunteer niche on the board of the German American Women's Club, where my language skills and familiarity with German culture allowed me to serve as a bridge of sorts between the Germans and American military spouses. The experience was both fulfilling and validating.

When I wasn't volunteering, driving the kids to school, soccer, or hockey (don't get me started on Jacob's hockey adventure, for which I had to learn to say "athletic cup" and other equipment terminology in German), or taking day trips with the other spouses, I planned our family trips. We had only three years of what I considered playtime, and we squeezed every ounce of that sponge dry by traveling during the kids' school breaks and American holidays when Mark's office was closed.

As soon as we returned from one excursion, I immediately started planning the next, barely able to savor the previous adventure we'd just had before crowding the memories out with dreams of the next destination. Maxing out my artistic license account, our trip scrapbooks show only beautiful scenes and happy faces. A subliminal message to my children runs through each and every page: *You WILL remember that you had a happy childhood; you WILL remember that we showed you the world; you WON'T remember that I yelled a lot, especially when you had a fistfight with each other while waiting in line at the Vatican or when you pretended to wrestle in the showrooms of Venice's glass masters.* Now that I think about it, I did include a photo of them fighting in front of the Vatican.

Unlike my garden in Virginia, my temporary garden didn't call out to me in the midst of my comings and goings. Having yearned for years for more flat space in my property at home, our plot on the military base was perfectly flat and, quite frankly, boring as a result. I was like a man with a skinny girlfriend who missed the curves of the woman who left him. Mature trees shaded the entire backyard to the point where only moss would grow. Fixing it would have taken years, so I was off the hook. I was back in my nomad state of mind.

Rather than getting my gardening fix at home on the base, I wandered through majestic palace gardens and admired quaint village window box displays in country after country, taking notes and photographs for future inspiration. The penultimate garden nirvana experience was spending an entire day on my own exploring the Chelsea Flower Show while Mark chased the boys through London. For years, "Chelsea" had carried the same mythical aura for me as "Disney" did for children around the world. I never imagined I'd ever get there to experience the magic for myself. As I joined the thousands of other gardeners making their way along city blocks of vibrant floral displays, edgy landscape designs, and commercial vendor stands, I felt like an impostor. A happy impostor, but an impostor nonetheless. I would never come close to having the gardening mojo that comes with England's horticultural history. There was my ego again, telling me I wasn't good enough! I laugh when I think about it now.

Our flat yard in Stuttgart did come in handy for one important event. A couple of weeks before his eighth birthday, Jacob asked if he could have a food-fight party. Birthdays had been an opportunity for my otherwise sports-centric sons to express their creativity to the hilt. Both boys took ownership of their parties, from theme development to cake design to the planning of activities. I'm not sure what I was feeling guilty about when Jacob suggested a food-fight party, but there must have been something going on since

I agreed without hesitation, with the caveat that it needed to be outside.

It was the one and only time in my life that I cooked mashed potatoes from a box. They didn't taste as bad as I had expected. More importantly, the weird potato flakes provided a cheap and easily prepared ingredient for the arsenal. We made trays of dense Jell-O to cut into cubes. We filled bowls with frothy whipped cream sprayed from chilly cans. A string tied across the middle of the yard was the dividing line between the opposing teams. You had to throw your ammunition but hold on to the pots and bowls (bringing a mashed potato- and Jell-O-covered kid to the emergency room for stitches was not on the list of activities).

Just before we let the kids loose with the food, I had a panicky moment of *What was I thinking?* But the hilarity of the ensuing scene overcame any second thoughts. Mashed potatoes proved to be perfect for scooping up and throwing with little hands. The spuds had enough heft to cover some ground even if a kid's pitching technique needed work. The whipped cream was too light to throw very far, but the cherry Jell-O clumps were excellent ammo.

The kids wore disposable rain ponchos, so whenever a moving target was hit, you'd hear a satisfying "splat." My only oversight was not having the children go barefoot. I doubt the

Jell-O stains ever came out of their sneakers. After the party we sent Spirit outside to clean up the mess.

Despite its shortcomings from a gardener's perspective, our borrowed yard gave us what we needed most at the time— the freedom to roam and a perfect field for a food fight. And that birthday party gave me a taste of what it felt like to relinquish control of outcomes, no matter how messy: sheer joy.

PART II

Pruned

prune: *v.* 1. To cut off or remove dead or living parts or branches (of a plant, for example) to improve shape or growth. 2. To remove or cut out as superfluous. 3. To reduce . . . To remove what is superfluous or undesirable.

—The American Heritage Dictionary of the English Language, fourth edition

CHAPTER 8

Reentry

By the end of our three-year posting in Germany, it had become normal for the kids to ask how many stars our next hotel had. And whether breakfast was included.

It was time to get back to the real world.

And it was time to return to my garden. Between the breathless travel and social schedule we had maintained during our expat experience and my refusal to connect with my rental garden, I felt ungrounded. It had been three long years since my Virginia garden had calmed me down. Those negative energy zigzags revealed by the parenting class instructor were stronger and sharper than ever, at least in the privacy of my own home. And although I talked about gardens and visited gardens and helped friends with their gardens in Germany, my own garden there made me look like a fraud.

On the flight home, physically and emotionally spent from the packing process and many rounds of goodbyes (school friends, soccer friends, military friends, German friends), I pushed the recline button on my seat, closed my eyes, and wondered what awaited me in my garden.

The purple smoke bush stood more than fifteen feet high—three times taller than when I left—as awkward as an NBA basketball player sitting at a first-grader's desk. The ornamental grasses had become an overgrown thicket, having foregone their annual haircut for three years. The forsythia shrubs on the back slope were a tangled mess of leggy branches entwined with wild grape vine and English ivy. The conifers flanking the front portico had grown much too fat in our absence, obstructing the view of the front door. (I had put on some girth myself.) The foundation shrubs had inched up enough to block most of the sunlight that used to stream through my living-room windows—the same sunlight I had missed desperately in our dark and shady home on the military base in Stuttgart. And the Japanese maple at the corner of the back patio stood brittle and leafless, or, to use another word, dead. Apart from that, things didn't look too bad.

Before I could get to the massive pruning job required in the garden, we needed to take care of pruning back our possessions to fit everything into the house. We had acquired some new things on our travels, mostly in the category of pottery and table linens. (I didn't go as far as some of the military wives, one of whom shipped home fifteen crystal chandeliers.) We also had a moving-truck's worth of boxes that had been in storage for three years, which, with the exception of old photographs, I would just as soon have doused with gasoline and ignited.

Although I had missed the garden, I hadn't missed the house. All my attention during our first decade of home ownership had been focused on the garden. I realized that I didn't even like being inside the house. As a newlywed, I could never have imagined that 2,300 square feet of living space would ever feel small. But with each passing year, our clutter's footprint swelled until it filled every nook and cranny. I didn't want a bigger house. I wanted fewer things and more efficient storage space for what we did keep. The kitchen hadn't been updated since the 1980s, the tiny master bathroom was the original from 1973, and something about the entry from the carport to the house, the door we used 99 percent of the time, put me in a foul mood. Maybe it was because my knuckle jammed into the door frame every time I turned the key in the knob. Instead of "Ah! I'm home," my usual exclamation when entering my house was, "Shit! My knuckle!" And although the perpetually open wound finally scarred over during our three-year escape, any thought of coming home and walking through that door made me cringe with anticipated pain.

The house itself, I realized, was part of my zigzag problem. Maybe if I were more comfortable inside my home, I wouldn't always be looking for reasons to leave it. Even when I was working on a paid project with the kids occupied elsewhere, I was more likely to take my laptop to a coffee shop since "home" felt so unsettling.

Mark and I talked about moving, but the prospect of another house hunt was as appealing to me as looking for another nanny. Besides, property values in our area had skyrocketed in the intervening years, and we wouldn't have been able to afford something better in our school district. Most importantly, I was ready to get back to my garden, which, unlike the house itself, soothed and fed my soul. The garden could sustain me while we fixed the inside spaces.

I started reading up on kitchen remodeling and space organization. Somewhere along the way, I stumbled upon a book about feng shui design concepts. I didn't know anything about the principles of "wind and water" (the literal translation of feng shui), but I had heard of chi, the energy from nature, and it seemed from my quick perusal of the book that feng shui had something to do with maximizing the flow of positive chi in your environment. Hmmm . . .

Already nodding in agreement as I read about the impact our surroundings have on our internal well-being, I gasped when I read about the importance of doorways: the chi in the house will suffer if doors "squeak, stick, have broken latches or handles too close to the edge so we scrape our knuckles whenever we open them."[5] *What???* I had been cursing that poorly placed doorknob for ten years. Why hadn't I delved into Chinese philosophy sooner?

The doorknob was only the start. I learned that clearing clutter plays a central role in feng shui, with a heavy focus on the link between internal order and external order: Cluttered house = cluttered mind. Orderly house = orderly mind. Jamming my knuckle on the doorframe, tripping over something left in the hallway, not being able to find things in piles of papers or laundry, all of it produced negative chi. And while the book included complicated charts about Chinese astrology and different types of baguas (energy diagrams to assist with design and placement decisions), there were enough practical solutions that I could implement on my own without having to get into anything too woo-woo. I was still an economist, after all.

So when the moving truck with our long-term storage boxes arrived, I went into high gear. Another garage sale was first on the list, followed by Craigslist sales, runs to Goodwill or other charities to donate what didn't sell, and, my new favorite clutter-clearing device, Freecycle,[6] which is like a giveaway version of Craigslist aimed to reduce landfills.

A strong infrastructure at home oozing positive chi would prepare me for my next chapter, I reasoned. My volunteer work in Germany had reminded me how fulfilling engagement with a team on a purposeful project can be, and I thought I felt ready to reenter the working world. The boys hadn't seen their mother earn a paycheck for three years or experienced the trade-offs that come with that. References to Mark being the wage earner in the family were cropping up with disturbing frequency, which made me grind my teeth.

And besides, the boys have had it too easy with you as a full-time mom, my ego muttered in my ear. *Since life itself hasn't intervened to force them to become as independent as you were at their age, you need to take matters into your own hands. They need to be ready in case anything happens to you or to Mark. And by not having you around so much, maybe they will appreciate you more.*

The bullying ego voice was relentless. I bought into it. If my nine- and twelve-year-old sons weren't going to stroke my self-esteem daily with their gratitude (because that's how all young boys behave with their mothers, right?), then I would just have to go out and find that somewhere else. But first, my closets and file boxes needed organizing so that the kids could find things when I was at the office, even though a paid job was still a figment of my imagination.

And so I had a plan. After the moving boxes were unpacked and Freecycled, I dove into networking and took on some contract work to get my foot back in the door. The simple act of dressing like a professional again for informational interviews and networking lunches made me feel important. My ego cheered me on, telling me, *There you go! That's what you're supposed to dress like! That's why you got your master's degree! That's what being a responsible, contributing member of society looks like!*

Meanwhile, we jumped back onto the spinning carousel of northern Virginia travel soccer, which entailed multiple practices for both boys each week and games each weekend, pretty much year round. Jacob decided he wanted to try lacrosse as well, adding a second sport to his spring agenda. Our carpool schedule rivaled the complexity of a military deployment flowchart.

Although I was usually preoccupied while driving carpools with how I was going to meet a contract deadline or on where I should focus my next networking attempts, shuttling vanloads of boys to sports practices was one of my few sources of intel. As long as I kept my mouth shut, all sorts of priceless information about girls, embarrassing voice-cracking moments, and school pranks would bubble up to where I sat behind the wheel. I wasn't ready to give that up.

But it's YOUR turn now, Martha, my ego would shout in my ear. *It's time for YOUR life to start. Let somebody else do the driving. The boys are practically grown men. They're way too dependent on you. In some countries they'd be responsible for their own goatherds by now. Look at how self-sufficient those kids in* Slumdog Millionaire *were. Don't you want your kids to be that resourceful? It's time for you to go back to real work like any self-respecting, educated woman would do!*

But that wasn't part of the plan.

CHAPTER 9
The Mammogram Callback

The tiles felt cold through the seat of my jeans as I sat with my back propped against the locked bathroom door. Cody knocked and announced that he was going to a friend's house. "Okay," I said, raising my voice a little too high to camouflage my tears. The Kleenex box on the floor next to me was almost empty, but the toilet paper roll was still half full. I could pull from that if needed.

I dialed Alice's number, half wishing she wouldn't pick up. Her "Hello?" came through the line amid a tangle of background noise. She was loading her kids into the car to get to soccer practice, embroiled in the usual mayhem of "Do you have your ball? Water bottle? Watch the muddy feet!"

"Oops," I said, "bad timing. I'll call you later."

My friend of twenty-plus years could hear that something was wrong. "What's up?" she said, refusing to let me escape.

I took a deep breath and quickly blurted out, "I had a follow-up mammogram a few days ago and the radiologist basically told me she thinks I have cancer."

"Oh, Martha," Alice said.

Her sympathy dissolved the semblance of strength I had tried to maintain since the radiologist had given me the news. The mammogram detected three abnormal clusters of cells, or "calcifications," that hadn't been there in my previous scans. The radiologist was concerned about one of them, but the lab would biopsy all three just to be on the safe side.

As I choked the story out, Alice somehow managed to stay totally present with me even while helping with seatbelts and soccer bag storage. She continued to console and reassure me on the other end of the line until Jacob discovered my hiding place.

"I can't find my athletic cup!" he wailed. We were leaving in a few minutes for his first lacrosse practice. The cup was required for him to play, making this a real emergency.

The athletic cup crisis cut my conversation with Alice short. I drove my cupless son to lacrosse practice, met the new coach, offered to help as a team parent even though I had never seen a lacrosse game in my life, and explored carpool options with another mom. Then I rushed to the sporting goods store, where I stood in front of a hundred athletic cups and asked the poor guy helping me, "How does somebody lose an athletic cup?" What I really wanted to ask him was, "Do I look like someone with cancer?"

I bought the one-size-fits-all cup (foreshadowing many future conversations about cup size of another sort) and raced back to the field like an ambulance driver, all the while thinking to myself that one in eight women gets breast cancer. If I could do this favor for my mother and sisters and girlfriends to reduce their statistical chances of getting it, I could handle it.

Or could I?

Having navigated through some rough waters during my childhood, my adult life had been pretty smooth sailing. I had spent years waiting for the other shoe to drop, and now it had.

"It's my turn to have something crappy happen," I told my sister, pragmatically. My greater concern was how everybody else would take it. Processing my own worry was hard enough. The thought of having to process other people's worry sapped my dwindling reserves of energy.

Telling my mother, who had just lost her husband, was my biggest concern. Fearing that she would disintegrate with the news, I decided to postpone burdening her until after I had the biopsy results. (It turns out that I couldn't have been more wrong about my mother, who, besides Mark, became my strongest pillar of support.) We also held off telling the boys.

The radiologist had explained in detail why she was so concerned about the largest of the three calcifications. In effect, she told me point blank that she thought I had cancer. But without biopsy results, nobody would believe me. "False positives are so common" is the usual response when you tell people you failed your mammogram. But I knew in my heart the doctor wouldn't have been so direct with me if there were any question.

I cried myself to sleep silently the first few nights after the radiologist's assessment, imagining my children without a mother on their graduation and wedding days, as I had been without a father on mine. Cody, having just turned thirteen, was the same age as I was when my father died. I knew what it felt like to be looked upon with pity by clucking neighbors and whispering friends. I didn't want my children to have to carry the burden of their mother's illness, and perhaps even her death, either outcome staining the fabric of the rest of their youth. I knew that my chances of dying were minimal at such an early detection stage, but I could not yet take ownership of that logic.

Imagined scenarios starring my motherless children filled those first few nights. The following days were marked by physical and emotional numbness, uncontrolled onsets of tears, and the heavy weight of raw, cold fear in the pit of my stomach. I hadn't learned yet that I had the power to pick and choose which thoughts deserved my attention. I immersed myself in a pool of imagined suffering even before I received the biopsy results.

Along with the fear and a very foreign feeling of desperation was a sharp-edged sense of resentment, as uncomfortable as swallowing a tortilla chip without chewing it enough and feeling it scrape its way slowly down your esophagus. Just when I felt I had been gaining a little bit of momentum toward my life's next chapter, life jammed a stick between the spokes of the wheel.

Biopsy Day arrived on Friday, April 13, as luck would have it. The plan was to attempt a stereotactic core needle biopsy, an office procedure in which the radiologist removes the targeted tissue with a hollow needle. The doctor had warned me, though, that my small breast size would make this method more difficult. The fallback would be a surgical biopsy at the hospital.

A quick word on my breast size: in the eighth grade, my friend Susan and I had decals ironed onto t-shirts that read "Proud Member of the Itty-Bitty Titty Committee." She eventually grew out of that status, abundantly so. I never did. As the only small-breasted woman in my family, my nieces' growth milestones were not marked by when they grew taller than their aunt, but when their bra size exceeded my A cup. Oh, the irony. It seemed to me that if you're given tiny breasts (even tinier after having breast-fed two babies), you should at least get a pass on cancer.

"I've heard that they're doing amazing things with reconstruction now," Mark said as we sat in the radiologist's waiting room. I laughed it off, telling him that we wouldn't have to make such a drastic decision. If it did turn out to be cancer, I assured him, it would be at a stage too early to require a mastectomy.

My name was called and I kissed Mark goodbye, wondering for the first time whether he had secretly wished all these years that my breasts were bigger. Inside the procedure room, the technician instructed me to lie facedown on the table, which had a hole through which my breast hung in all its diminutive glory. A mammogram machine was clamped on. The paddles squeezed. When they had the calcifications on the screen a few feet from where I lay, I tried not to read too much into it when the radiologist said to the technician and nurse, "Look—right there." The two women murmured in response, "Oh yeah" and "Wow."

Wow? I'm lying right here, people. I don't think you're supposed to say "wow"!

The needle used to pull the tissue sample for the biopsy is very long. As the radiologist had explained at our last appointment, the breast tissue needs to be thick enough for the needle to be inserted properly, otherwise you stand a good chance of being shish-kebabbed. I dubbed this procedure the boob-kebab.

They tried everything to grab enough critical mass. I faced one way on the table. They spun me around to face the other way. They moved the mammogram machine every which way. "Can you pull some tissue from my butt?" I asked. No, but they did try to pull some from my neck. No go. Finally, the radiologist made the call: I was officially too small-breasted for the stereotactic biopsy method.

Plan B was a surgical biopsy to be conducted by the breast surgeon at the hospital.

More consultations and pre-op tests required me to cancel scheduled networking meetings and put new contract work on hold. I kept up with my carpool driving commitments, but not without unexpected onsets of tears that I wiped away before anyone noticed.

At home, I continued my feng shui clutter-clearing efforts, which included researching contractors for the kitchen remodel we were finally ready to undertake. And although the energy in the house had, indeed, started to improve with my nascent organizational improvements, cancer fueled the grumbling ego in my head: *This was supposed to be the start of your next chapter!*

The garden was the only place I could be open and honest with my emotions. My fears and frustrations were met with silent acceptance, no empty reassurances were offered up, and my only concern was making sure my gloves didn't smear mud across my face when I wiped away the salty evidence of my sadness.

I had assumed the surgical biopsy would be less involved than having an ingrown toenail removed. I was surprised, therefore, when the surgeon we had chosen at the renowned Georgetown Hospital in Washington, D.C., told us that the procedure entailed general, not local, anesthesia. I wasn't worried about that from a medical standpoint. Medical procedures, hospitals, and anesthesia didn't frighten me (doctor's daughter, remember?). It did change the calculation, however, of waiting to tell my mother about all of this until after I had the biopsy results. I realized that if the tables were turned, I would be angry if she didn't tell me she was having surgery. What if by way of some fluke I didn't wake up? She'd kill me.

The full title of the procedure I would be undergoing was a surgical biopsy with core needle localization. When suspicious lumps or abnormal cells are identified in the breast, surgeons need pointers to make sure they are removing the correct tissue to test. The procedure to insert the pointers is called a needle localization.

The surgeon explained that, prior to the surgery, the hospital's radiologist would insert hollow needles into my breast while I was clamped into a mammogram machine, then wires would be threaded through the needle to mark the abnormal clusters for the surgeon. She explained all of this matter-of-factly, with no hint that I would experience any discomfort.

During my pre-op check, a hospital technician suggested I ask my breast surgeon for a Lidocaine patch for pain management. My surgeon complied, but said the patch wouldn't help much, since it numbed only the skin and didn't reach deeper tissue. She explained that, in the opinion of the Georgetown radiologists, deeper pain medication distorted the reading and complicated the placement of the needle.

I applied the patch the morning of my procedure and hoped for the best. Women went through this all the time, I thought to myself. It was the twenty-first century, after all, and we were in the United States, home of the best medical care in the world. How bad could it be?

I was the model patient as the technician clamped me into the hospital's mammogram machine prior to the surgery. The radiologist introduced himself and asked, "Are you alright standing up? It makes the reading easier."

"No problem!" I said, determined to remain cheerful and helpful throughout.

The paddles squeezed and the image appeared on the screen, magnifying the calcifications. A cold numbing agent was sprayed onto my skin and the radiologist thrust the first needle into my breast. I sucked in my breath and saw stars. With the second needle, I felt I had been transported to a medieval torture chamber. By the third I had fainted (for the first time in my life), and the radiologist had to bear-hug me from behind because I was still clamped into the mammogram machine.

Each of the three calcifications needed at least two needle pointers properly placed, which sometimes required repositioning after the needle was in. Once a needle was positioned correctly and the wire was threaded through its core, a picture was taken. The radiologist tried to make me feel better by saying that men would never be able to withstand this or the pain of childbirth. "Every woman knows that," I told him. "You'll have to do better than that."

A few more fainting spells and an IV-drip later, the nurse wheeled me, crumpled and tear-streaked, to the operating room for the biopsy surgery. I couldn't wait for the anesthesia to carry me away. A year later I would learn that different doctors have different approaches to pain management during the needle placement procedure, and this—among the most hellish experiences of my life—might have been avoided if I had asked more questions.

At our appointment to hear the biopsy results, eight long days after the tissue was taken, Mark and I waited in the exam room. When the surgeon and her resident walked in, I saw the answer on their faces. The surgeon started talking immediately, in a rip-the-Band-Aid-off-fast approach.

"The news is not good," she began. "All three calcifications are malignant. It's *ductal carcinoma in situ,* which is noninvasive, officially Stage 0. But they cover three quadrants of the breast, in which case we usually recommend mastectomy with reconstruction."

I stared at her blankly. Even though I had prepared myself for getting the "you have cancer" news, I had only expected one of the three clusters to test positive based on the radiologist's initial read of my mammogram. But the possibility of a mastectomy with early-stage breast cancer had never entered my mind. How much time would that take?

My risk of dying from cancer was minimal, given how early we had caught it. That risk was about the same whether I had a mastectomy or lumpectomy, the doctor explained. But if I chose to go the route of lumpectomy, or more accurately three lumpectomies (the surgical removal of a wider expanse of tissue where the calcifications had been), I would be left severely deformed. Large-breasted women might get away with it, but I would have next to nothing left. Even worse was that I'd need six weeks of daily radiation following the lumpectomies. Six weeks worth of doctor's appointments was unimaginable to me. I would not let cancer rob me of that much time when my life was waiting to start. At least chemotherapy wouldn't be needed since we had caught the cancer before it became invasive. I would suck at chemo. I am so prone to nausea that I have thrown up after doing a U-turn driving my own car. I knew my system wouldn't tolerate toxins being pumped into my body, so I was deeply grateful that chemo was off the table.

The breast surgeon wrote out a referral for an informational appointment with Georgetown's chief of plastic surgery. All of this happened within a matter of minutes after having been told that I did, indeed, have cancer, not just in one area, but in three.

Getting a boob job had always been at the top of my lengthy "things I'll never do" list, even higher than living in the suburbs and owning a minivan. I had been very outspoken about it, in fact, especially when I felt surrounded by bobbing double-D buoys on the military base in Germany. Just a couple of years earlier I had surveyed my fitness trainer at the base's gym and a masseuse at an American-run ski resort, asking them if a lot of their customers had implants. Both of them confirmed that breast enhancement was popular with military spouses. When I thought about it, I realized that I had a few civilian female friends in my address book who had pumped themselves up as well, so maybe generalizations were unfair. Lying comfortably on my stomach while the masseuse kneaded my back (one of the perks of small breasts), I said, "I just can't understand why anyone would feel a need to get plastic implants to improve their body image. They're so fake!"

"I agree," she said. "But what about breast cancer survivors and reconstruction? What are your views on that?" I had never given it any thought.

"That would be different, I guess," I replied sheepishly. I preferred to keep my holier-than-thou thoughts focused on how sad it was that so many women bought into the advertising industry's definition of "normal" or "beautiful" when it came to breast size.

I insisted to myself and others (the topic came up surprisingly frequently at expat women's happy-hour gatherings) that I was glad my breasts would never hang down to my navel and that they weren't a hindrance during exercise. Besides, improvements in bra technology meant that you could always find a boost at Victoria's Secret for special occasions.

Faced with the prospect of a mastectomy, I had the option to skip reconstruction and instead be fitted for a prosthesis bra cup-filler. Plenty of women went this route, uncomfortable with the idea of implants or other means of fabricating breasts. Many breast cancer survivors choose to forego any form of false advertising.

As I debated whether to opt for reconstruction or not, my first thought was that there hadn't been much there in the first place. I probably wouldn't miss the thing. I didn't feel that my sense of my own femininity was closely tied to my modest mammary glands, which had already served their biological purpose by then anyway. Mark said he would support whichever decision I made, and I believed him.

The flashback to my conversation with the American masseuse in Germany led to an even earlier memory. It was 1987, and I was visiting my mother's sister not long after her own mastectomy. I was in my early twenties. My aunt, at fifty-six, was a successful social worker who had gone back to school after her kids were grown to earn her master's degree. She was an avid gardener, rarely missed her daily water aerobics class (and still doesn't now that she's in her eighties), and approached life with a no-nonsense, just deal with it, attitude. In short, she was (and is) one tough cookie.

We had gone to her club for a swim. As I was getting dressed in the small, curtained cubicle afterward, lost in thought about how all swim-club dressing rooms smell the same no matter where in the world they are located, I heard my aunt weeping in the stall next to mine. I dressed quickly and went to her.

I found her with one strap of her bathing suit off, the rubber prosthesis only partly covering the angry red scar slashed across the flat plain where her breast had been.

"I just can't get used to seeing this," she said through her tears. I embraced her and let her cry.

She told me later that breast reconstruction methods and technologies were still very new at the time of her cancer diagnosis. Inserting the rubber prosthetic mound into her bra and bathing suit has been part of her morning routine for more than twenty-five years. But there's no getting away from the naked truth in the mirror, no matter how good you look in your clothes. Although I had yet to become fully aware of how the universe was working to guide me in my journey, the memory of that scene in the dressing room with my aunt somehow gave me permission to say yes to reconstruction.

CHAPTER 10
They Can Rebuild Her

"Look," I said to Mark. "There's the Box O' Boobs." I pointed to a stack of clear plastic drawers stuffed with silicone breast implants in the corner of the plastic surgeon's exam room. It looked like a jellyfish colony. As we waited for our informational consult to begin, the Box O' Boobs stared me down, the most recent manifestation of "This was never part of the plan."

My mind was already reeling just from the waiting-room experience. The décor featured before-and-after photos of nose jobs and tummy tucks, and brochures for liposuction were stacked in neat containers next to women's magazines. I wished I had a sign that read "I have cancer. Why are you here?"

Mark and I were still weighing treatment options. Mastectomy seemed like overkill since we had caught the cancer so early, but I couldn't get the Elephant Man's cry of "I am not an animal!" out of my head whenever I thought about the misshapen mess my breast would be after three lumpectomies.

Just as important, if I chose lumpectomy, I couldn't envision how I would fit in six weeks of radiation treatments to zap the little bit of breast tissue that would remain. With the boys' school and sports schedules crowding the calendar, not to mention my own efforts to jumpstart my career again, I was determined to give cancer only as much time as was required, and not a minute more. My priority was to get my life back in order as quickly and efficiently as possible. I figured that six weeks of radiation would certainly take longer than simply snipping off the breast. Characterizing this short-term perspective as totally naive would be an understatement.

On the day we received the biopsy results, the breast surgeon had explained briefly the two types of breast reconstruction. The first is implants, which can be made from a variety of materials—saline, silicone, or a rubbery substance with the consistency of gummy bears, though the gummy option wasn't fully approved when I was making my decision in 2009. The second reconstruction method uses the patient's own tissue to form the new breast, moving it from either the belly or back.

The breast surgeon didn't think my body type supported moving my own tissue around, which in any case would have entailed a much longer and more painful recovery process.

Many candidates for this procedure find that the longer recovery is worth it, however, since the end result usually looks and feels more natural. We would have to wait for the plastic surgeon's assessment of my options.

Before our first consultation, I had perused the plastic surgeon's website, which included a gallery of before-and-after shots of reconstructed breasts. Would I be asked to pick which ones I liked best, like choosing from a rolling cart of dessert plates? Is that what the Box O' Boobs was for? Although my aunt's experience made the prospect of reconstruction more acceptable to me, my previous judgments about breast enhancement were still very much alive. I didn't want to look noticeably different because of cancer, even if the difference would be "better" by society's standards. It felt wrong and inauthentic to me, as if I were just using cancer—and only Stage 0 cancer at that—as a ruse to keep up with the Joneses. After all my ranting over the years about the shallowness of breast enhancement, I would be selling out.

The plastic surgeon's resident—young, blond, and wearing a white lab coat and killer heels—arrived first. She explained again that reconstruction would either entail implants or moving tissue from other parts of the body.

My big question was how the reconstructed breast would compare to the original on the other side. I imagined myself ten years from now, my artificial left breast defying gravity, while my tiny right breast, literally deflated, hung southward. At the resident's request, I flashed my robe open.

"Oh," she said. "I can tell you right now, we can't make it look like that."

"Why? Too small?" I asked.

"Basically, yes," she replied. "We would augment the healthy side to make it as similar as possible."

I was surprised to learn that insurance would cover this. The Federal Women's Health and Cancer Rights Act of 1988 mandated that insurance companies cover mastectomy surgery and reconstruction of the cancerous breast, as well as surgery on the other breast to "produce a balanced and symmetrical appearance."[7]

The bottom line was that, if I did choose mastectomy with reconstruction, the medical order would include a boob job on my healthy side as well. At least that would give me a face-saving way to tell my friends and family that, after forty-five years as a member in good standing of the Itty-Bitty Titty Committee, I would no longer be eligible.

The resident went on to explain that, because I wouldn't need radiation (which can damage tissue and complicate reconstruction procedures), they could start rebuilding me as soon as that pesky cancerous breast was removed. Once the breast surgeon and her team had completed the amputation (which was how I later came to view the mastectomy), the plastic surgeon would ride into the operating room on his white horse to save the day. I'm paraphrasing a little.

The resident told us that the first stage of reconstruction with implants is to insert a "tissue expander" between the rib cage and muscle. The expander, which is sort of like a folded up rubber ball, is slowly filled with saline in increments over three to four months. She may have used the rubber ball example, but I think it's more like Jiffy Pop Popcorn foil tops that balloon to accommodate the popping kernels. The expander stretches the skin and muscle to create an opening, kind of like digging a hole big enough for whatever sized root ball you're planting. Once the expander has been filled to approximately the size of the new breast, a final surgery switches out the placeholder for the not-so-real deal.

I was following the resident's explanation until she started talking about the pig tissue. It goes something like this: in some cases, after the breast is removed, something needs to help hold the expander in place so that it doesn't slip around while everything is healing. You wouldn't want to wake up and find that the thing had slipped to the middle of your chest, after all, or around to your back, or down to your knee.

My eyes glazed over and I literally had trouble catching my breath after she mumbled that the tissue they use for this comes from either a human or a pig. *Huh?* I told her I had some Jewish ancestry. Though this is true, I am not observant and eat loads of bacon. I was only trying to buy time to get my heart rate down.

Her boss strolled in at that very moment. In response to my aversion to being a pig-tissue host, he said, "It's no problem. The rabbis have cleared on it. I think they even bless the tissue before it goes out." The resident chimed in that the tissue was washed "really, really well" to make sure that no genetic material was left. Great. The first test subjects probably grew curly tails and cloven hooves.

It felt good to have something so well-defined to be mortified about, when the rest of my emotions seethed below the surface, unprocessed and pulled in a thousand different directions. At the same time, laughing at the absurdity of it all was my way of staring cancer down, mocking it—even when the joke was on me.

Now that the plastic surgeon was there, the real exam began.

"Okay, let's take a look," he said. I held my robe open, feeling like a flasher. He grabbed my stomach fat and confirmed that I didn't have quite enough there to use my own tissue for the reconstruction, especially in the event that cancer was found in the healthy breast and they needed to deal with that side, too (a comforting thought that hadn't crossed my mind up to that point). I asked the same question I had posed in the unsuccessful first biopsy attempt: could they pull tissue from my butt, where the bulk of my fat was stored? He said it was possible, but the tissue comes off the very top and it leaves a little shelf.

I imagined serving martinis from my butt shelf while simultaneously holding out a tray of hors d'oeuvres to my guests. Always looking for efficiencies, I saw some benefit to the system. Mark was less enthusiastic.

The doctor said, "May I take another look?" I opened my robe. "You know," he quipped, "every woman I've ever asked has shown me her breasts. No one has turned me down." He added with a glint in his eye, "You know how they have Take Your Child to Work Day? My friends want to come to work with me every day."

Everyone has her or his own relationship to humor, especially during a crisis. Personally, I rely on it to diffuse tension. I laughed at the doctor's jokes and was grateful that he had helped keep things light, even while recognizing that some women—especially other cancer patients—might have found his wit terribly offensive. From an economist's perspective, expending energy on feeling offended was an inefficient use of my resources. I didn't know it at the time, but using economics logic to decide whether or not to feel like a victim isn't all that different from mindfulness techniques.

We finalized our decision to move forward with the mastectomy, but the surgery wasn't scheduled for several weeks. We had visitors arriving from Germany who had planned their trip months in advance of my diagnosis, and the doctors said it was safe to wait until after their departure. It was good to keep busy while entertaining our guests, but it didn't leave me much time to think about what lay ahead.

Paid work was put on the back burner, with doctor's appointments seeping into what had previously been time slots for networking. Cancer was taking not only my breast but also my productivity, the latter more central to my sense of self.

In an effort to thumb my nose at the diagnosis, I told Mark that I wanted to move forward with renovating the kitchen. The house and I would be reconstructed all at the same time, and I would feel as though something had gotten done even when I wasn't earning money.

The little bit of free time I had before the first surgery was spent in the garden. It was the height of the spring planting season, but I knew I wouldn't be able to tend to anything too needy in the coming months. Planting my dahlia tubers was a priority. Knowing that I had the promise of those saturated blossoms in the fall helped me look beyond the difficult days that lay ahead. Weeding became more than weeding. I discovered myself clawing and stabbing at the earth with my trowel, gritting my teeth as I unearthed the roots of invasive, unwanted plants like so many cancer cells.

The doctors had explained that I wouldn't be allowed to lift anything for a few weeks after each surgery. Mulching was my presurgery act of defiance. Lifting and carrying dozens of forty-pound bags of mulch to spread over all of my freshly weeded beds gave me a feeling of empowerment that I hoped would carry me through my days of confinement. I lugged countless gallons of water from my rain barrels to my planting areas, water sloshing over the edge of my bucket and splashing my feet as I climbed the back slope again and again. My hope was that an extra big drink of water before my first surgery would tide my plants over if it didn't rain during my convalescence.

Although I wasn't yet conscious of the connection, the physical exertion involved in these "hard labor" projects and the sensory experience of tending the plants (the silky feel of hydrangea petals, the porcupine feel of purple coneflower seed heads, the cinnamon scent of cranesbill geranium) crowded out the crazy-making thoughts that filled my head whenever I remembered that I had cancer:

But you don't really have cancer! It's only Stage 0, my ego would say. *Even though the doctors say you have cancer, your cancer doesn't measure up to other people's cancer! If you had Stage 3 or Stage 4 cancer, then you would really deserve some attention. If you had Stage 3 or Stage 4 cancer, and really had to worry about the prospect of dying, then you would deserve a new pair of boobs.*

Emotionally, I was so caught up in my confusion over whether I should feel good or bad about coming out of cancer with larger, lifted breasts (would I still be "me" or something plastic and less credible?) that I didn't give much thought to the mastectomy itself. Since I had never relied on my breasts for my self-esteem or sense of femininity, I didn't think that losing one would be that big a deal. I was getting rid of the cancer, literally, disposing of it, which was all that mattered. I was also in decent physical shape, so I didn't worry too much about the recovery period. In my head, the math was simple. A couple of surgeries and a few days of recovery versus six weeks of daily radiation appointments and the potential for scary side effects, not to mention the constant worry about whether the cancer would reappear in my deformed Elephant Man breast.

Mark and I tried to stay focused on the positives, first and foremost the very early stage at which the cancer was detected, but also the improvement in my profile that recon-struction promised.

Enjoying an al fresco dinner one evening in Washington, D.C., the sidewalk traffic served as a perfect runway stage. "What do you think of those?" I asked Mark, nodding in the direction of a woman walking by in a tailored white blouse.

"Those are nice," he said. "What size are they?"

"Probably about a C cup," I guessed.

A fit-looking woman passed by in workout clothes, small-er-chested than the white-blouse model but still shapely up top. "I like hers," I said. "I think those are a B. Yeah, probably a B. I'd be perfectly happy as a B."

Mark and I both stopped chewing our food at the sight of the next woman, a plus-sized model in tight pants, four-inch heels, and a low-cut red t-shirt that strained to control some of the biggest breasts I had ever seen. The woman's cleavage started at the base of her throat. I couldn't begin to guess what size they were. (How high do bra cup sizes even go?) Mark looked at me inquisitively.

"Absolutely not!" I answered.

The Amputation

The morning my mastectomy was scheduled, I woke up with the burning realization that I had a urinary tract infection. The presurgery restrictions on eating and drinking had most likely exacerbated the symptoms, providing a painful diversion from thinking about the surgery even as we drove to the hospital.

Tests confirmed an infection, leading the plastic surgery team to get cold feet. Risk of infection is always a concern with reconstruction, even without a preexisting source somewhere else in the body. The doctors decided to go forward with the removal of the breast, but postpone phase I of reconstruction (insertion of the tissue expander) until a few weeks later. The potential for gangrene wasn't appealing, I agreed.

Finally, the breast surgeon simply said, "Okay, let's go."

I got out of my chair and we walked—yes, *walked*—in parade formation into the operating room. Along the way I was handed a puffy cap to put on. Was that a dirge I heard playing somewhere in the background? Was I dressing myself for my own execution? I climbed onto the operating table and lay flat on my back as instructed, all the while thinking, *Shouldn't I be asleep by now?*

"Arms out," someone said.

I was still much too awake, as the reality of what was about to happen finally began sinking in.

Part of my body was about to be clipped off. There was no other way to look at it. And although I knew that pruning my plants invariably spurred new growth, I couldn't begin to imagine that this would one day be true for me as well. As I lay on that table, all I could envision of my impending amputation was permanent loss. Sure, an implant would eventually fill the void, but a silicone substitute felt as garish and inauthentic as a plastic daisy on a stick purchased at Walmart.

As the nurse wrapped my arms in crucifix constraints, each arm immobilized at ninety-degree angles, leaving my breasts and the heart below them no room to hide, tears floated to the surface.

Wait! What if I don't wake up? The thought honestly hadn't occurred to me until I was strapped onto the table. I had written notes to the kids and Mark before going to the hospital, but I really should have given the possibility of death a little more consideration. Too late now.

The anesthesiologist was murmuring gently in my ear that they would keep me warm, etc., but I was fighting back tears and longing for the drugs to take over before I started sobbing. I was Velcroed into confinement and couldn't wipe my eyes or blow my nose. *Please, just don't let snot run out of my nostrils while I'm still awake!* Just as the first salty teardrops slid down my temples, a merciful fog engulfed me.

I woke up from the surgery surprisingly comfortable, with very little pain and having almost full range of motion in my arm. My chest looked about the same as it had before the surgery, with the bandages padding my left side to about the same size as the small, lonely breast on the right.

Had the tissue expander been inserted as had been originally planned, I would have woken up more visibly changed. Pain would have been more of an issue as well, with the expander wedged between my muscle and rib cage. So for a few minutes at least, I felt unexpectedly good, still looking and feeling like my old self.

Those first "glass is half full" thoughts didn't last long. The ick factor began to sink in as soon as I returned home from my one luxurious night in the hospital.

After my initial elation that I didn't have any real pain (I was sent home fully supplied with Vicodin, Valium, and Percocet, but I didn't need anything stronger than Tylenol by the second day), the truth behind the lack of sensation sank in. All the breast tissue, along with all the nerve endings, had been removed. The left side of my chest was scraped as clean as a Thanksgiving turkey carcass, eliminating any capacity for sensation where the breast had been. Moreover, a drainage tube hung out of a hole in my side, calling to mind my rain barrels' overflow hoses.

As the swelling declined over the course of those first few days, my ribs protruded more and I could feel the drainage tube snaking its way across my bones. There was a hollow area along the side of my rib cage where I hadn't realized breast tissue had provided a cushion for my arm, which now fell into a boney cavern. An involuntary "Eeww!" escaped my lips whenever my arm made contact with my skeleton. And that didn't even take into account the scar that stretched six inches across my chest and made half of me look like a nippleless ten-year-old boy. I had expected the scar, at least, which took some of its power away.

A deep numbness—the kind you get from Novocaine at the dentist's office—ran from my armpit down to my elbow. I had been forewarned of this potential side effect of the sentinel node dissection, or removal of some of the lymph nodes to screen for cancer cells. Sometimes the numbness is permanent if a particular nerve was inadvertently cut. It would be several months before I'd know whether I fell into that category. I didn't, but it took more than a year before the numbness had disappeared completely. In the meantime, shaving was treacherous and I lived in fear of exposing my armpit to open flames, which I didn't think my seemingly dead tissue would be able to feel. I kept my distance from lit candles and gas stove burners.

Despite my Stage 0 status, the pathology report confirmed that my cancer cells were fast-growing (so-called high grade) and aggressive. Staring at my scar in the mirror, I needed to believe that invasive cancer would have developed if we hadn't treated it aggressively. However, when I researched *ductal carcinoma in situ* (DCIS), I learned that it's an unpredictable type of cancer, sometimes becoming life-threatening, sometimes not. The crazy-making voice in my head ignored the pathology report, telling me repeatedly, *This surgery probably wasn't even necessary!*

In the three weeks between the mastectomy and the first reconstruction surgery, I cried myself to sleep more nights than not. Along with the discomfort and disgust I felt each time I touched or looked at the drainage tube hanging from my ribcage, I hated the constraints placed on my physical activity. I wasn't supposed to lift anything that weighed more than a few pounds. Even if I had had the doctor's permission, my body was too weak to carry out my normal activities. Simply drying my hair with my good arm proved exhausting, forcing me to sit down on the toilet halfway through the job. Weakness and dependency were traits I had feared since childhood, and I was now mired in both.

The garden called to me through the kitchen window, begging me to come out and play. Venturing outside in my bathrobe and slippers when nobody was looking, I dragged the hose around the yard with my good arm, quenching my plants' thirst where I could and apologizing to those that begged for more attention. I snipped some hydrangeas to cheer me up inside the house, arranging the pink, purple, and blue mopheads in a clear cobalt vase. Even the small act of bringing a few blossoms inside taxed my energy reserves, reminding me how spoiled I had been by my good health up to this point. I sucked at being sick.

Forced to simply sit down and wait until my strength returned, without the distractions of my previously stuffed-to-the-gills schedule, I found myself becoming highly sensitized to my environment. I could feel the flow of energy around me, both positive and negative. If the boys were arguing, I asked them to take it outside or simply went to another room to separate myself from their negative zigzags. Healing as quickly as possible was my objective, and I could sense at the core of my being that negative energy hindered my progress. Even phone calls from worry-filled family and friends had a negative impact on me, which led to Mark taking on the role of telephone gatekeeper. Flowers, on the other hand, boosted positive energy, so I carried my vase from room to room with me.

About a week after the mastectomy, the surgeon answered my prayers and removed the drainage tube. The sensation was akin to what a plastic lid must feel like when a straw is pulled through it. With my unpadded, hollow-feeling rib cage, I felt like the bride of the Tin Man. On the upside, I was elated to be liberated from the evil drain, which not only had kept me up at night from discomfort, but was also a constant reminder that a part of my body had been sliced away and discarded.

I celebrated my drain removal by having lunch with a girlfriend that day and taking Jacob to a doctor's appointment, trying to feel as if my life was getting back to normal. That evening, though, I saw that fluid had started to accumulate where the drain had been. When I checked in with the doctor the next day, I was told to wrap my chest in an Ace bandage to minimize swelling. Encasing my ribcage like a sausage in a tight skin put the finishing touch on my new identity of Least Sexy Woman on Earth.

Although I couldn't work in the garden—my normal means of escape—during this period, I could do research for my kitchen renovation. I was now more convinced than ever that structural improvements were crucial to maximizing the flow of positive chi in the house. The kitchen project soon broadened to include the family room, laundry room, and basement. My next surgery was coming up, and if I had to go back to ground zero with my physical activity, I wanted at least to hear workers transforming my house while I lay in bed doing nothing.

The plastic surgeon was concerned at my pre-op appointment that, despite my Ace bandage efforts, too much fluid had collected around the site of the incision, which could complicate installation of the tissue expander. As I stood before him in my usual flasher pose, he asked for a syringe to aspirate the site. Once again, not being able to feel the needle as it pierced my skin and sucked out the excess fluid was worse than pain.

When he saw the tears running down my cheeks, the doctor said, "Wow! You have beautiful feet!" I looked down at my feet and back up at him as though he had just escaped from a psych ward. Then I realized what he was doing.

"You're just saying that to distract me," I said. "They teach you that in medical school, don't they?"

"Well, yes," he replied. "But you do have pretty feet."

Let me say for the record that I do not have pretty feet. At least I didn't then. At the time of the compliment I had toenail fungus, scaly skin, and sandpaper heels. I thought back to our first consultation, when I noticed the resident's toe cleavage. I glanced over at the attending nurse's feet and saw that she, too, was wearing red four-inch heels. The man probably had a foot fetish. I guess his comment did serve its purpose, though. By the time I cleared my mind of images of fondled feet, he had pulled the needle out from under my skin, my boy chest sucked dry.

Three weeks after the mastectomy, just when some of my strength was beginning to come back and I was able to give the garden the attention it deserved, I went under the knife again to have the tissue expander inserted. As difficult as the intervening period had been, I was now fully convinced that reconstruction was the right choice for me. I didn't think I would ever be able to come to terms with the ripple of ribs where my breast used to be.

Aesthetically, the new "mound"—which filled my shallowly cupped hand—looked better than I expected. The muscles that had been displaced by the tissue expander hurt, but it was worth it. It was good even to feel pain again, as opposed to the creepy numbness that had dominated the left side of my rib cage after the mastectomy. Most striking was the immediate shift in my spirits. The mound provided a lift in every sense of the word.

Prior to the start of reconstruction, I had been feeling a little guilty that insurance would be paying for new breasts. Now, having a clear picture of the impact on my mental health before and after they started to rebuild me, I understood why breast cancer patients deserve to have access to reconstruction if they so choose. It was no different from insurance paying for a prosthetic leg or arm to help make us feel whole again, even if that wholeness isn't our own tissue.

The dreaded drainage tube was back, though, a literal and figurative pain in my side. The firmness of the expander and the awkward hose made it uncomfortable to lie down or sleep in any of my familiar positions. Sleeping on my stomach, as I had done my whole life, was like lying on top of a rock. I tried to pile pillows to make a hole for the breast to fall through, like those inflated donuts they give you to sit on after you've had a baby. Someone had recommended sleeping propped up in a lounging pillow with arms, the kind my grandmother used to have to watch TV in bed. It helped a little when I was still taking enough drugs to knock me out, but not after I finally pulled myself together and said no to the Percocet (a sad goodbye indeed).

About two weeks after the expander was inserted, my mother took me to my checkup with the plastic surgeon, where I was hoping to have the drain removed. The doctor and nurse debated whether my drainage volume was sufficiently reduced. Despite my deep aversion to the thing, I was worried about pulling the hose out too soon. I didn't want to have to bind my chest with an ace bandage again, or worse yet, have more needles stuck into me to suck out fluid.

In response to my concern, the smooth-talking doctor casually said he would "fill the space so fluid wouldn't be able to collect." I wasn't sure what that meant. Without further ado, he handed me an IV bag to hold, then proceeded to stick a needle through my nerveless skin into the tissue expander. I felt the bag shrinking in my hand and looked down to see a breast rising like Mt. Everest from my chest. My mother, who was also in the room, had a horrified look on her face. Later she said it was like watching me go through puberty in thirty seconds flat. It didn't hurt, but I became a little hysterical.

"What are you doing? What if I don't like it? Will it pop if I laugh too much? What if I sneeze?" I asked frantically and all at once.

He said anything could be changed later. He just wanted to make sure that there wasn't a void in which fluid could collect. He had injected 250 cubic centimeters (cc's) of saline into the 450 cc tissue expander.

"What if I want 700 cc's?" I asked.

"That would be like a Big Gulp drink," he replied.

After the doctor and nurse left the room, my mother said, "Hello, Dolly!" We were laughing so hard we were crying.

On the way home in the car I said, "If I start to float away, please grab my ankle."

CHAPTER 12

Reconstruction All Around

We signed the contract for the kitchen renovation thirteen days after my mastectomy and seven days before the first reconstruction surgery. If I had to put my physical productivity on hold, planning productivity could fill the void. My ego wouldn't let me get away with doing nothing at all.

Since a wall would be taken down to create an open floor plan, the kitchen renovation was really a family-room renovation as well. New wood flooring would extend the project to the foyer. The laundry room and carport entry were at the top of my list of negative chi sources (the knuckle-bashing door latch was just one of many issues), so I launched a full-court press on Mark to make the case for gutting that room as well.

My email correspondence with the designer and contractor, a gentle and extraordinarily patient soul named Ray, gives a clear picture of just how desperate I was to keep myself both distracted and productive following my mastectomy on June 10, 2009, and my first reconstruction surgery three weeks later. June 15: "Hi Ray. I'm up and about again after my surgery. Let me know when you would like to schedule an evening consult."

July 5: "Hi Ray. The renderings you emailed came through fine. I had another round of surgery this past Tuesday and am still regaining enough energy to review the design and perhaps discuss some more fine tuning."

August 11: "Hi Ray. I sent you our granite decisions last Monday on our way out of town. Now that we're back home, I'm noticing that the cut flowers I bring in from my garden each summer really clash with the Bordeaux granite we chose. Is it too late to make a change? I don't want to have to base my gardening decisions on my countertop color."

And so it went. It was a summer of doctor's appointments, chauffeuring the boys to soccer camps (including an emergency pickup when Cody got swine flu just days before my first reconstruction surgery), researching hundreds of options for doorknobs and drawer pulls, backsplashes, and faucet finishes. We had a storage pod in the driveway and a dumpster on the curb.

Noise, dust, and problem solving with contractors filled my time at home. But with each new change—old cabinets ripped out and thrown into the dumpster, decades'-worth of muck behind the appliances revealed and swept clean, faded and warped linoleum pulled up and replaced with gleaming hardwood—I could feel the energy in the house shifting. The space felt lighter, fresher, and full of possibility. Like a soldier at boot camp, my house (and, I came to see later, its owner) needed to be broken down to its most basic foundation before it could be built back up to reach its highest potential.

But why stop with the main floor of the house? Once the kitchen was far enough along that we could cook there again (a hotplate, rice cooker, and microwave oven served the purpose in the basement for a few weeks), my clutter-clearing ambitions extended to storage for our books, photos, games, and toys in the rec room downstairs. Not only that, the boys were entering their teen years and I wanted a hangout space that would be inviting for their friends.

When Mark balked at each new estimate of the ever-broadening scope of work, I implored, "But we're in the zone, now. I'm in decision-making mode, and since I can't take on new work right now anyway, this is the perfect time to just get it all done."

It's hard to say no to a cancer patient. We signed on for the basement renovation, covering the wedding costs for yet another of Ray's many children.

I was flying fully on intuition during this period, simply tuned in to what felt right or not right. As soon as the laundry room was cleared of its poorly designed, door-impeding closet and light flooded in where the appliances had formerly blocked the windows, I felt elated stepping into my home from the carport (with knuckle skin intact), even when the room was still just a shell of drywall.

The same was true of the basement. Though I wasn't yet at the point of looking at each room from a feng shui standpoint, I later learned that, like smoke, energy rises. Whatever is collected in your basement has an impact on the energy throughout the rest of your house. Feng shui experts recommend removing objects from your basement that you never use in order to keep healthy energy circulating underneath you and to provide a strong, supportive foundation. This must have been what was driving me as I carried box after box from the basement to the storage pod in the driveway in advance of the basement's demolition, the beginning of which corresponded with my final surgery.

My last reconstruction surgery—my fourth time under the knife that year—was scheduled for October 28, three days before Halloween. An email arrived about a week prior to that from my girlfriends Yoon and Felice, who were both living in Africa at the time. Felice lived in Zambia, but was visiting Yoon in South Africa. Yoon wrote, "Since we're together, we've had too much time to plot. We've sent you a little gift. Check your mail in the next day or two."

A package arrived from Amazon. I pulled out a clear plastic packet stuffed with shiny blue and white polyester fabric. Fringe and stars peeked through the folds. It was a Dallas Cowboys cheerleader costume. I cried with gratitude, not because I'd finally have breasts for the first time that would fill out this ridiculous outfit, but because I was blessed with such supportive and loving girlfriends. Felice followed up with an email that read, "Know we are thinking of you and sending you all the positive karma from the Southern Hemisphere to add to that coming your way from the Northern Hemisphere. You have the planet covered."

As I lay in bed after returning home from the hospital, the sounds of hammers crashing against nails, power drills buzzing, and circular saws screaming through wood beams were like a lullaby. Now that I think about it, the Percocet may have played a role as well.

CHAPTER 13
A Hard Look at Habits

My body had been pruned. My house was being pruned. But it didn't stop there. Shortly after my first reconstruction surgery, I met with yet another doctor at Georgetown Lombardi Comprehensive Cancer Center to talk about what I could do to stay healthy. Dr. Priscilla Furth, a physician-scientist and professor of oncology and medicine, specializes in understanding how cancer develops and improving strategies for prevention. She explained why pruning some areas of my lifestyle would reduce my risk of recurrence.

I thought the breast would be the only thing I would lose. Soon after my diagnosis, however, they told me I would need to stop taking Wellbutrin, the antidepressant I had depended on for years, because it made the breast cancer medication Tamoxifen less effective. Although I took only a low dose, I felt I needed that pill to take the edge off my genetic predisposition to the blues. I could try switching to another family of medication, but the prospect of dealing with new side effects was more than I could handle at that point.

And then there was the alcohol. As we interviewed various doctors to decide on my team and treatment plan, the question of how much alcohol I consumed was on every questionnaire. We had just returned from three years in Europe, where wine was a staple not only at dinner, but often at lunch as well. Even our German American breakfast gatherings always kicked off with a bubbly flute of Prosecco. Mark and I had started a small wine collection and had brought several cases back from Europe, extending the magic of our expat days over dinner in Virginia. I didn't think twice when I filled in the space on those medical forms with "one or two glasses of wine a day." (Although my intake had declined since our return to the States, I was probably still low-balling it.)

Dr. Furth explained that alcohol consumption does, indeed, increase a person's risk of developing breast cancer, but I was unaware of it. Not wanting to believe her (all she had was a Yale and Harvard medical school education and thirty years' experience), I looked it up at home. The National Cancer Institute's website confirms that "more than 100 epidemiologic studies have looked at the association between alcohol consumption and the risk of breast cancer in women. These studies have consistently found an increased risk of breast cancer associated with increasing alcohol intake."[8] Shit. My prevention doctor, as I came to think of Dr. Furth, told me that no alcohol would be best, but, like a child who gets a "no" from one parent and runs to the other, I asked my oncologist. She was a little more lenient, but still wanted me to keep my intake to two or three glasses of wine a week. *A week.* I have some very large wine glasses but, sadly, I was limited to four ounces per drink. I could have used that Wellbutrin when I got the news. Or a sixteen-ounce glass of Malbec.

Dr. Furth had more good news when she told me that exercise would reduce my risk of cancer recurrence. She put me on a treadmill for a stress test and was impressed with how quickly my heart rate returned to normal levels after a mild cardio workout. "That means your heart is healthy!" she said, which sounded good at first, until she explained that I would need to engage in really intense cardio exercise to get the cancer risk reduction benefit she had told me about.

"I was thinking about signing up for a Pilates class," I told her.

"Pilates is nice," she said diplomatically, "but it won't be enough for you. Walking won't be enough either. You need to have your heart rate above 140 beats per minute for at least 30 minutes most days of the week. Preferably every day. You'll need to work up to it." Shit.

In the early days of cancer treatment, fear is the motivator. I had dodged a bullet. Just thinking about my close call, beads of sweat sometimes broke out on my forehead, especially when I looked at my pathology report that contained terms like "High Grade" and "Aggressive." And once you've had cancer, you're automatically bumped into a higher risk category for getting it again. Now that I had the information about alcohol and exercise, I couldn't ignore it. Ignoring it would be prioritizing old habits over being around for my kids' weddings. Not acting upon the information that the doctor had provided me was not an option. But I resented this new demand on my time. High intensity exercise was yet one more thing I *had* to do as opposed to what I *wanted* to do, which was to move on to my next chapter. The exercise requirement would be there for the rest of my life, which was pretty damned daunting.

I bought a heart-rate monitor and joined a local gym. I had always hated running and hoped to get my cardio work taken care of on the elliptical trainer, stationary bike, or rowing machine. The good news was that the thirty minutes didn't need to be consecutive, so I could break it up between different types of exercise. Ten minutes on three different machines didn't sound too bad, but I learned that it took a few minutes to get my heart rate up to its target range during those lower-impact activities, and I lost ground when moving between the machines. My workout was taking much longer than the thirty minutes I was willing to give it.

Wanting to get it over with as quickly as possible (would I ever have time to garden again?), I begrudgingly got on the treadmill and started jogging. I couldn't jog a mile. I couldn't jog half a mile. I couldn't jog for five minutes without needing a walking break. Sure, it was only a few weeks after my first reconstruction surgery, but with no history of running, this was my authentic starting point.

I used to tell people that I didn't run because I was allergic to it. When I had tried running in the past, my skin would start to itch from my thighs all the way up my torso. I couldn't stop myself from scratching, which made the itch even itchier. At the end of a run, I looked like I had been mauled by a tiger. Heat and humidity—the hallmark of Virginia summers, which is when I was embarking on my new fitness regimen—intensified the problem, so I surrounded myself with fans on the treadmill at the gym.

I looked for any excuse to stop. My hair bouncing on my head drove me to distraction. Tying it down with a headband helped. Hats made me too hot, especially after the Tamoxifen I took brought on hot flashes. My nose ran constantly so I clutched a handkerchief for nose-blowing. Wanting to be anywhere other than where I was, music or an audiobook playing in my ear helped keep me going, but the earphones were a constant annoyance. Keeping water close at hand helped squelch my fear of collapse, so a water bottle had to be either jammed into the treadmill cup holder or, if I was trying to run on the road, held in my non-nose-blowing hand. I spent a small fortune on high quality, sweat-wicking running clothes, telling Mark my life depended on it. I was as sensitive a runner as the princess who could feel a pea under a stack of mattresses.

But I kept going. And slowly, step-by-step, it got a little less hard. The itching calmed down. I wrestled my hair into submission. I was prepared for a runny nose. One by one, I eliminated the excuses not to run (except that even though it was less hard, it was still hard). If I felt I deserved a break, or if I just couldn't motivate myself to lace up my shoes, I asked myself, *Is there a really good reason not to go?* In other words, *Is there a really good reason to risk not being at my kids' weddings?* Every so often there was a real reason, but usually not. Because the truth was, I had started to feel good after running. Never during the run itself, mind you, but afterward, without fail.

My wine habits evolved as well. At the oncologist's suggestion, my new policy was to drink only if I socialized with friends on the weekend. Like the running, I had to work up to this. In the beginning, I would measure out four ounces of wine (with an actual measuring cup!) and walk around holding the glass, alternating between small sips and breathing in the bouquet. Slightly pathetic, but my strategy worked. In fact, it didn't take too long to realize that holding the glass or simply having it nearby was almost as satisfying as actually drinking the wine in it. I understand now why smokers who are trying to quit sometimes walk around with unlit cigarettes between their lips. More often than not, there was still wine in the glass by the time I went to bed. The flip side was that since my wine quota was so small, the quality of that wine had better be worth it.

And although I had always been a fairly healthy eater, I now had to look at nutrition as a cancer survivor. This presented a whole new field of research—much of it contradictory—that I dove into when I wasn't parenting, chauffeuring, exercising, visiting doctors, or working on house renovations. Words like "antioxidant" and "free radicals" used to be mere marketing buzzwords, but now I had a vested interest in learning how what I ate might affect my cell structure (specifically how antioxidant-rich foods can reduce concentrations of cancer-inducing free radicals in the body). It seemed that everywhere I turned a new study popped up. Chemicals in meat that was fried or cooked at high temperatures on the grill increased your cancer risk. Green tea reduced your risk. Broccoli and cauliflower (and the rest of the cruciferous vegetable family) reduced your risk in one study, but showed little correlation to cancer in other studies. Coffee was deemed bad in one book I read, but it was okayed by my oncologist. I love my oncologist. For reasons that were not yet fully apparent to me, the importance of exercising my body and making healthy nutrition choices seemed to go beyond merely reducing my risk of cancer recurrence or improving my physical appearance. But I couldn't yet put my finger on why.

CHAPTER 14

The Garden Epiphany

Despite my neglect, the garden kept growing.
Years of soil amending and careful planning to place the right plant in the right spot paid off the year after my mastectomy, when healing, house remodeling, and educating myself on cancer prevention absorbed all my time and energy. The woody shrubs, in particular, held things together, starting with the flash of yellow from the forsythia in March to the soft pink and heady fragrance of the Mohawk viburnum in April to the blues, lavenders, pinks, and whites of my various hydrangea cultivars starting in June. My frenzy to get my dahlia tubers planted before my early summer surgery was rewarded when, despite the heavy blanket of weeds at their feet, a rainbow of luxuriously textured blossoms put on a show from late summer until autumn's first frost. The depth of joy those dahlias gave me that year was like another form of oxygen.

After giving cancer and contractors a year of my time, I was ready to get back to work on my life again, that elusive next chapter that kept inching its way from my grasp. But the dance with cancer had taught me a few things. Time is fleeting. My kids were growing up at warp speed. I liked being there when they got home from school. I still wanted to work and earn an income, desperately so, but a nine-to-five office job was off the table for the time being. I took a grant-writing class, hoping to add that skill to the broader writing and editing services I marketed on a freelance basis. The work didn't light a fire in my belly, but the paycheck validated something that needed validating at the time.

Finally, I pulled on my faded denim overalls and headed back out to the garden, where I could strategize. So much needed to be done in my wild garden beds that it felt akin to embarking on a long run. And with that voice in my head still muttering about what my life "should" look like *(You should be wearing a suit, not these ridiculous overalls. You're healthy enough now. Stop being lazy and find a real job!)*, a knot started to form in the pit of my stomach.

In search of distraction, I decided to listen to an audiobook while doing the mindless work of weeding. My online supplier (Audible.com) had recently had a big sale, and I had downloaded several books to keep me company while running, with only a quick perusal of the titles. Scrolling down the list of options on my iPod, I clicked on *A New Earth: Awakening to Your Life's Purpose* by someone named Eckhart Tolle.[9] I had never heard of him, but job advice for $5.95 while I gardened sounded like a good deal to me. The thing about audiobooks is that you don't see the cover, or the "Oprah's Book Club Pick" sticker. If I had seen that sticker, I probably would have turned up my nose and moved on.

Audiobooks are usually read by professional actors, but the narrator of this one was far from that. He spoke excruciatingly slowly with a distinct German accent, no emotion whatsoever, and lots of strange pauses. *(Hurry up, already, I kept thinking. I don't know what to do with myself when you pause like that.)* But the first few sentences in the book are about the first flower that opened on earth 114 million years ago, so he had my attention from the get-go. I hunkered down into the weeds and dug in with my trowel.

"Seeing beauty in a flower could awaken humans, however briefly, to the beauty that is an essential part of their own innermost being, their true nature. The first recognition of beauty was one of the most significant events in the evolution of human consciousness,"[10] Eckhart read.

Hmmm. Maybe this was not the book I thought it was.

Listening to Eckhart talk about the evolution of human consciousness, posing questions about our capacity to defy materialism and rise above our identification with ego, the bad-boy voice in my head responded, *Is this a* Saturday Night Live *parody of a German psychoanalyst? When do we get to the part about how you're going to earn a bigger paycheck?*

Awakening to the beauty of the world around us right this very moment was at the heart of Eckhart's message. At first glance, this didn't seem that hard to do, especially while I was in the calming embrace of my garden. But the "awakening process" to which he referred soon crept into uncomfortable territory when the word "spiritual" started to pop up with increasing frequency. I was on a roll with the weeding, though, so it was easier to just keep listening.

As Eckhart described it, understanding the workings of ego both in ourselves individually and in society as a whole is central to this so-called spiritual awakening process. Within all of us there is "self" and there is "ego." Ego is what makes us compare ourselves—what we do, what we have, how we look—to others. These things have nothing to do with who we really are. Most of the blather in our heads is the egoic mind and shouldn't be trusted. Egoic thought clutters our head with content that doesn't serve us, precluding conscious awareness of our true essence.

Don't listen to him! shot back my egoic mind. But a deeper awareness within me was able to see that dynamic for the first time. My true self understood exactly what he was talking about.

Most of us spend our lives waiting for the next thing to happen, thinking that the next acquisition or experience will make us whole. Yet always looking forward to the next thing (in my case, my "next chapter") prevents us from being able to appreciate the moment we are in. Being fully present in the moment allows us to experience inner tranquility, recognizing that this moment—no matter what we have, what we are doing, how society views us—is the best moment there has ever been. Only in the present moment can we take action, not in the past (which still controls so many of us) and not in the future (which is just a set of imagined scenarios).

Finally, toward the end of the book, Eckhart provided the career advice I had been looking for in the first place. Our purpose in life is to do that which we find fulfilling and do it well. Whatever it is that we are doing in a given moment, doing it well in a highly conscious state of being is our purpose.

I stood up in my muddy overalls, my trowel dropping out of my gloved hand into the dirt. A deep sense of peace washed over me, unlike anything I had ever experienced before.

Although Eckhart's frequent use of words like "presence," "consciousness," and "spiritual" initially took me outside my comfort zone, I realized that I had been told to pay attention to these matters twenty years earlier, but the advice had fallen on deaf ears.

When I was twenty-five years old, exactly half a lifetime ago at the time of this writing, my sister had my astrological chart analyzed as a parting gift when I was moving from Seattle to Boston for graduate school. Mae, the chart reader, explained her findings in a face-to-face meeting and recorded our conversation on a cassette tape (the best of late 1980s technology).

Astrology had never been my thing, and most of the reading was foreign-sounding to me at the time. I frankly didn't understand most of what Mae was talking about. She used the word "conscious" a lot, defining the term as self-awareness and awareness of how we're connected to everyone and everything else in the world. In Mae's world, the evolution of the species depends on humanity's ability to learn to live more consciously.

As she talked about my particular planetary configuration based on the date, time, and location of my birth, something resonated. She said my life would be an ongoing cycle of chaos and order. I had already recognized that trend—which was still weighted heavily on the chaos side of the equation at that point in my life. But that could apply to a lot of people. She also said that I had already learned how to operate in the working world in previous lifetimes, which explained why work came easily to me. And she said that travel would be transformative for me, a means of higher learning. That was good, since at that point I planned to travel nonstop the rest of my life.

Totally ludicrous, though, was when she said, "Your particular chart configuration shows that your purpose in life this time around is not about career." *Excuse me? I'm about to haul my ass to the other side of the country to start graduate school!* The chart said that career was old business I had already learned how to do, so it wasn't my task in my current lifetime.

According to Mae's analysis, my journey this time was supposed to be a spiritual one. I nodded politely and stared with glazed eyes at the strange symbols scattered across the chart diagrams, but what I was really thinking was, *Sorry, don't think so. I have much more important work to do.*

"Your goals have to do with developing yourself in a way in which you are very much in the present. You're not in the past and not in the future. Your realm is the present. Your success will depend on how fully present you are in the moment. Your success doesn't depend on work and your destiny doesn't come from your work. You're not creating a product or concept for the world. Your whole thing here is to reevaluate yourself, be very aware of yourself. Your survival is going to have to do with presence. Does that ring a bell in any way?" Mae asked.

"Yeah, sure," I lied.

"Ultimately for everyone the ego needs to be sacrificed later in life in order for people to become a functioning part of society," Mae continued. "Let go of your ego and start to do it for something that's larger than you. In sacrificing the ego, that's when you really get to offer your wisdom and serve mankind. At that point the serenity and peace that comes out of this part of life is available to you. Your whole chart is set up to push you to that awareness before other people tend to come to it."

My twenty-five-year-old ego replied, *Who needs serenity and peace? How boring! Are you really listening to this airy fairy crap?* "These configurations force you inward to a more spiritual mode and upward."

What the heck?

Although I had dabbled in Christianity in high school, I was totally turned off to organized religion by the time I hit college. Religion had simply caused too much damage in the world—war, intolerance, violence against women, and utter hypocrisy—for me to be a fan. I believed in a higher intelligence of some kind, but I was by no means religious. I wasn't even very curious, and I never would have described myself as a spiritual seeker. Still under the false impression that "spiritual" meant the same thing as "religious," my guess was that Mae had her planets slightly misaligned. I felt bad that my sister had wasted her money.

After listening to the cassette several times over as I drove from Seattle to Boston, I still wasn't any closer to comprehending it by the time I reached my destination. I packed the tape away and forgot about it while I completed my master's degree and embarked on the life of exciting work and international travel that I fully believed to be my purpose in life.

Years later, when our nanny's surprise departure pushed me off the career ladder, I recalled Mae saying that my focus this time around wasn't supposed to be career, and I applied this information like a salve on the wounds of my identity crisis. The other details of the reading, however, dissolved into the ether.

My confusing conversation with Mae came flooding back to me as I listened to Eckhart explain the difference between "spiritual" and "religious." Spiritual awakening begins when we recognize the mechanics of ego in ourselves and in society as a whole, specifically ego's role in turning everything into us vs. them. All religions point to a similar truth, whether we call it salvation (Christianity), enlightenment (Hinduism and Buddhism), or the end of suffering (Buddhism). These and other religious traditions have the transformation of human consciousness—the realization that all of us stem from the same source and are therefore inherently connected—at their core. But eventually, ego turned these seeds of truth into ideologies that fed our false sense of self, making us right and all those "non-believers" wrong.[11] He managed to explain in clear terms what I had been thinking ever since I was sixteen years old, when, as an exchange student in Turkey, I met some of the loveliest, kindest, and most warm-hearted people I had ever come across, who just happened to be Muslim. Those people weren't going to burn in hell just because they weren't Christian. If they did, I'd be happy to be there with them at the party.

When Mae had used the word "spiritual" in the chart reading, I had immediately associated it with either church ladies or crystal-carrying incense burners. But the problem lies in the semantics. A simple word, which is just a construct of vowel and consonant sounds, can never fully convey the depth of the universe. Language is too limited, too imperfect.

I recently replayed Mae's cassette tape, which first required unearthing from my storage room an ancient boom box covered in dust. Mae's soothing voice came through the static, interrupted every couple of minutes by my twenty-five-year-old self's nervous laughter. I wonder whether Mae had sensed just how awkward I felt. I wanted to reach back in time and give myself a reassuring hug.

Once I got past the sound of my ill-at-ease voice, what I heard made me laugh out loud: "It says here that home may play a big part in your life. Finding a place you can call your own and personalizing it in some way could be very important to you wherever you go," Mae said.

Although I have no recollection of this part of the chart reading, I probably thought at the time, *Home? When would I ever have time to focus on where I keep my clothes? I'll be too busy exploring the rest of the world!* If she had suggested that gardening might play a part here, I would have rolled my eyes and groaned right then and there.

And then this . . .

"Your configuration will require you to learn to love yourself," Mae said. "It will require you to give up judgments about yourself like 'I'm not x enough,' 'I'm not y enough,' 'I'm not smart enough, courageous enough, fast enough,' whatever it is. Oh, and one that's not going to work for you is 'I can't do this because society doesn't value that.'"

"I don't usually think that," I replied, adding more confidently, "that's never really crossed my mind."

Guess I spoke too soon.

They say there are no accidents. If I had been any other place than in the garden, not wanting to stop working to pull off my dirty gardening gloves, I would have switched my iPod to another audiobook choice. Instead, Eckhart Tolle's words streaming through my headphones led to an epiphany so deep that, for a brief moment at least, my ego was silenced for the first time in my life, pruned from my thought process. Utter tranquility ensued in that moment. And nothing would ever be the same again.

PART III

Blossoming

blossom: *n.* 1. A flower or cluster of flowers.
2. The condition or time of flowering . . .
3. A period or condition of maximum development. . . . *v.* 1. To come into flower; bloom.
2. To develop; flourish . . .

*—The American Heritage Dictionary of the English
Language,* fourth edition

CHAPTER 15

Awakening

I don't know how long I stood still in the garden that day, my feet rooted among the flowers as the rest of my being was liberated of a burden I hadn't realized I had been carrying. For the first time ever, I felt I had permission—if not some sort of cosmic urging—to be truly happy simply being where I was.

I had not been looking for spiritual enlightenment and didn't even have the language at the time to explain what was happening to me. In fact, I was decidedly uncomfortable with the "spiritual" label. But the only way I could describe what I was experiencing was that I had apparently forged a connection to a higher intelligence, pure consciousness, perhaps even the source of creation. It was a little embarrassing, as far removed from my former sense of identity as were the house in the suburbs, the minivan, and the bigger bra size I now wore beneath my gardening overalls.

Shining a light on ego—the source of my resistance to each unexpected turn of events—allowed me to look back on my life with new clarity. I hadn't been ready to hear the message of my astrological chart reading when Mae had presented it two decades earlier, but things played out just as the chart had predicted. I wouldn't have quit my job if the nanny hadn't skipped town—an earth-shaking crisis at the time—but now I couldn't be more grateful that she had. And I wouldn't have been capable of hearing these deeper truths emanating from my heart if breast cancer hadn't forced me to step off the chaos carousel, clear my calendar, and recalibrate my life.

A deep sense of purpose engulfed me, far more intense than anything I had ever experienced during my previous professional life. In this blossoming state of awareness I could see that everything in my life had happened for a reason, both the good and the bad. Each step had been required to lead me to this point of conscious awakening. My energetic connection to the garden now extended outward to the universe as a whole. I could feel, sometimes palpably, that I was (and am) part of a bigger picture, intertwined with everything and everyone around me.

This was why my negative energy had infected my kids (and anyone else with whom I came into contact), and why positive energy was contagious as well. Being a net producer of positive energy would be not only a gift to my family, I realized, but also its own form of community—and even global—service.

Exposing the workings of ego and recognizing my connection to the whole of creation was like throwing water on the Wicked Witch of the West, with the result that the judgmental, critical brain chatter in my head dissolved into a steamy puddle. And in that stillness, the beauty of the present moment came into full focus.

In those early weeks of what I now view as my awakening process, I went through my days in an almost too-present state, bumping into walls with my headphones on while listening to everything Eckhart Tolle had ever written,[12] barely speaking to those around me. My family and friends weren't quite sure what to think. I didn't take phone calls, didn't return emails. Nothing seemed very important in comparison to this bigger truth I had just discovered. Everything around me was fleeting, myself included. The stillness inside me was so completely calming that I avoided anything that would disrupt this state of peace.

The TV news was a fire hose that blasted pain, suffering, and conflict into my space and straight through my skin. I stopped watching it. I could still take National Public Radio in small doses, because the absence of visual images muted the energy. Email and social media felt noisy and overwhelming, not to mention thoroughly unimportant.

If the boys came in carrying upsetting energy individually or between the two of them, I experimented with simply listening and directing my presence toward them in an attempt to dissolve the negative vibe. Sometimes I sensed a lightening of their emotional load that seemed connected to this practice, but results were inconsistent. Even when I wasn't successful in calming them down on the spot, avoiding my usual reactivity still went a long way toward not adding to the drama of the situation. Things settled down a lot more quickly as a result. If I felt my ego reacting, I would leave the room (or sometimes even the house).

One of the earliest lessons I took from Eckhart's teaching was to reframe how I thought about "problems." We tend to infuse the word "problem" with drama and negativity, when in reality each life event is better thought of as a "situation." His simplified sound bite "There are no problems, there are only situations" clicked with me, since I was now able to see how things in my life that appeared to be bad had actually led to good things (new circumstances, rewarding experiences, greater insight). Drama simply wasn't necessary, no matter how hard ego tried to stir it up.

Sound bites aside, choosing to approach an event as a "situation" doesn't minimize its difficulty. And I'm certainly not saying that the widespread poverty, violence, and discrimination faced by millions of people around the world shouldn't be taken seriously and acted upon. Indeed, accepting the reality of "what is" doesn't mean that we have no control over our personal or collective situations. We've been given these incredibly powerful minds and bodies for a reason: to improve ourselves and, by extension, our planet and the universe as a whole. Our task is to take action where we can, hopefully inspired by the deeper truth available to us rather than our ego-driven thinking. And after we've taken that action, we need to step back and let go of the rest. It won't be long until the next step of a conscious course of action becomes clear. Until that time, why create more suffering for yourself by getting carried away by energy-sapping worry and drama?

From an economist's standpoint, it's a very efficient way to live your life.

What was missing at this stage of my process—the early days of learning the art of presence—was empathy. When someone told me about something that had upset them, my first response (sometimes to myself and sometimes out loud to them) was, "How important is it in the greater scheme of things?" If I could feel the other person's drama energy infecting my space, I would either remove myself or advise them to not fan the flames of the situation with their own reactivity. Because I was still highly sensitive to other people's energy,

I took action to limit my exposure to negative emotions. Sometimes that meant disengaging quite abruptly.

I sensed that people close to me became reluctant to tell me about their problems because I didn't provide the sympathetic ear they hoped for. "Don't let the negative situation have power over you," I would tell them. "Let go of what you can't change." This seemed like obvious advice from my new perspective, but it took me months—close to a year, perhaps—to realize this was easier said than done for most people. Eventually, however, as that raw sensitivity softened a bit, I learned to empathize in a way that gently neutralized some of the other person's emotional response. But in the beginning I probably came across as dumping cold water over the heads of whoever might be seeking a shoulder to cry on.

I made an effort to stop lecturing my kids so much and listened to them in a neutral, nonjudgmental state of awareness. Their first response was, "Why are you just staring at me? Say something!" Cody was probably right when, over dinner one night, he expressed frustration with me for "not taking anything seriously enough."

My new state of being in those early days not only influenced my outlook on life, but cut to the quick of my personality. I had been known for my sarcastic, impulsive style of banter, often accused by my children as "having no filter."

Observing each and every one of my thoughts and reactions so closely during this period revealed to me that my sarcasm and sometimes mean-spirited joking came from my ego center, whose objective was to make me look better than other people—smarter or funnier or simply not to be messed with. For a little while, I became so monotonic that I barely recognized myself. I believed I couldn't be funny anymore. Zen monks weren't usually portrayed as yucking it up, right? (That was before I saw the Dalai Lama in action, whose delightful sense of humor is what makes him so likeable and connected to his audience.)

As I expanded my research on other people's spiritual awakening processes, I learned that I wasn't alone in going a bit overboard those first few months. Eckhart Tolle spent two years living on a park bench after his awakening process had been triggered (he obviously didn't have to drive anyone to soccer practice).

A shout-out to Mark for his patience and adaptability while I was in my iPod-wearing zombie phase those first few months. Not only was he going to work and paying the bills, but he stayed on top of scheduling requirements when I couldn't see more than a few minutes in front of me.

As much as I might have wished to be sitting cross-legged on a mountaintop with no distractions from the present moment, the closest I could get to that was a few minutes in the garden—still the source of greatest connection for me— squeezed in between carpooling, cooking, laundry, my cancer-mandated fitness program, and the boys' soccer games.

Of course, the garden had been trying to awaken me all along. I realized now that the sensory experience of working the soil, feeling the breeze on my cheeks, inhaling the fragrance of a rose, even my muscles straining to lift a shovelful of dirt—all keep me grounded in the present moment, calm, tranquil, and content. Worries about the future or mulling over the past dissolve in an instant when I'm digging in the dirt. The garden channels all my energy into the here and now, the only place where anything real happens. Only later would I come to learn that there was a term for this present moment awareness: mindfulness.[13] Mindfulness has, in fact, been studied and practiced in eastern cultures for centuries, but I had never heard of it.

Happy, no doubt, that I was finally able to hear her whispers, the garden took me by the hand and helped me to hone my presence skills further. In the jumble of my overgrown garden beds, the process of assessing which sprouts were weeds and which had the potential to bloom paralleled that of observing my thoughts and tossing out those that didn't serve me well. The more space I created around beneficial plants—digging out chickweed between clumps of phlox and black-eyed Susans, and the more space I created around beneficial thoughts and ideas—discarding grumpy mutterings from my ego, the more my internal and external gardens were able to flourish.

It's not always easy to tell a weed from a flower. In the early stages of growth, you need to be able to recognize the shape of a leaf, the design of an edge, the form of a stem. The same is true for thoughts. A mental microscope is needed to determine if a thought is fear-based (ego) or truth-based (deeper consciousness, or source intelligence).

You're not putting your graduate degree to work! Yank that thought and toss it into the weed bin.

Your friends are getting promotions at work and you're earning nothing! Yank that thought, laugh in its face, and toss it into the weed bin alongside the other one.

What do you even "do"? Are you kidding me? Yank that most ridiculous thought and pile it onto the rest of the unproductive thoughts that ego devises to make us suffer. And let's go ahead and burn that pile.

Thought weeding created space for truth to bubble up to the surface. What were the sources of my deepest fulfillment? Being a mother. Gardening. Writing (but from the right-sided, noneconomist part of my brain). Why was I forcing the issue of maintaining a professional identity when it wasn't a financial necessity? It was fear that I wasn't living up to what I thought society expected of me, or what I had formerly expected of myself. Pruning reinforced my practice of being present. And after a year of the cancer-induced neglect of my garden, my clippers had their work cut out for them. The Annabelle hydrangeas required particularly intense focus, having grown into a witch's hair tangle of old and new growth. Since the shrub blooms only on new growth, each branch needed to be assessed. Was it new? Was it old but healthy? Was it dead? Some looked dead but revealed green living flesh beneath the papery surface when scraped with a fingernail. Old growth was sturdier and helped support the bulbous white blossoms on the new growth, so some should be saved. Slow work, not to be rushed. Inch by inch, branch by branch, some semblance of order emerged. Each cut created spaciousness for air to flow and new growth to spread. Each cut cleared my own head a little more.

Buddhists talk a lot about gardens, including the lowly compost pile. Though not a Buddhist myself (I'm still of the mindset that no single manmade framework encompasses all truth, and I'm not in need of a label), the connections drawn in Buddhist writings resonate with those of us who like to plant things. More than one Buddhist teacher has noted that, by alchemically transmuting forms of things into other forms, composting proves that nothing really dies. Energy is simply recycled into new life forms, new life cycles.

My own compost heap had a few things to say on these matters. Like everything else in my yard, my little compost bin had been left to fend for itself since the mastectomy, recovery from which did not lend itself to turning decomposing yard waste or putting it to use.

I had placed a catalogue order to fill in some holes where plants had perished during the year of my cancer treatment. A unique coreopsis cultivar, delphinium, phlox paniculata, and several other new introductions would be arriving soon. Heading over to the hidden corner of my side yard where my compost bin is tucked away, I hoped to find a supply of nutrient-rich soil amendment to plant with the incoming recruits. Since it had been so long since I'd last visited, I had no idea what I would find.

Removing the lid, I stabbed my pitchfork through the crusty top layer. I could have sworn I heard an "Ahhhh . . ." of relief as I lifted that first forkful of wormy black compost from its confines.

As I harvested the decomposed soil that had been created by the grass clippings, fallen leaves, and kitchen scraps of the previous year and began to build a new pile to begin the process all over again, the conversation really got going. We had quite a lot in common.

Compost: "Ahhhh. How wonderful to breathe again. Are you breathing?"

Me: "Yes, I'm breathing."

Compost: "No, I mean really breathing, with full focus. Feel the air flowing into your nose, filling your lungs, streaming back out again through your nostrils. Where do you feel the movement of breathing? Notice the rise and fall of your chest, your stomach moving in and out."

Me (stopping for a minute to pay closer attention to my breathing): "Wow. That really clears my head."

Compost: "Can you give me some water? I've been parched for months. Really slows my work down here. Are you drinking enough water?"

Me: "Probably not. I'll work on it."

Compost: "Don't forget to layer the brown stuff and green stuff when you're building me back up again. Are you layering enough into your life, mixing things up a bit?"

And so it went. The compost reminded me that I didn't need to micromanage, the proof being the thick layer of decomposed soil below the crusty surface, even though I had done nothing over the previous year to aid in the process. My guilt was assuaged. Ambitious composters can get caught up in the minutiae of how to speed up the timetable. Various ratios of carbon (from brown, dead stuff) and nitrogen (from green, fresh stuff) in the mix will determine how hot a pile becomes and, therefore, how fast it decomposes. But none of this is necessary if you're not in a hurry. Nature will figure it out, even if you aren't there fussing over every detail. This lesson pertains to gardeners and parents alike.

"Many roads lead to the same end," my new dirt pointed out to me. There is no single "right" way to get there. Compost bins come in all shapes and sizes. You can build your own structure with boards and chicken wire, or buy a stackable system or rotating tumbler. Or you can just dump a pile of leaves or grass in a corner and come back to it in a few months. As an old Chinese proverb says, "There are many paths to the top of the mountain, but the view is always the same."

"Draw from the past to grow in the present," my compost reminded me. Compost is the ultimate example of putting old stuff to work to nourish new growth. Our life journey works the same way. Each past experience is its own lesson for the future, as long as we're conscious enough to look for the kernels of wisdom at the bottom of the heap.

"Remember," the compost whispered, "beauty can eventually arise from the muck." This is a good lesson to hold in your heart in the midst of dark times. You might be bogged down in a life situation that feels like a slimy mix of coffee grounds, vegetable peels, and rotting leaves, but with time, patience, and self-reflection, positive transformation awaits.

You don't have to be a Buddhist to get the point. Bette Midler, who is known not only for her incredible stage talent but also for her advocacy of community gardens and green space protection in New York City, put it this way: "My whole life has been spent waiting for an epiphany, a manifestation of God's presence, the kind of transcendent, magical experience that lets you see your place in the big picture. And that is what I had with my first compost heap."[14]

As I worked black compost into the soil around my plantings that season, my own epiphany under my belt, I felt primed for growth. The question was how I would take the compost scattered along my own path and use it to bloom.

CHAPTER 16

Sound Body

My feet hit the pavement like a metronome, with an easy, automatic regularity. I've taken a side street to extend my normal running loop, trying to push beyond the three-mile mark that has become a little too easy.

I have left the iPod at home today. Without the earphones tuning out the world, I am amazed at all there is to hear. Birds vie for my attention with leaf blowers and barking dogs. The breeze sets in motion the rustle of leaves overhead and cools me, deepening my connection with the world around me. A shaft of sunlight flashes upon a drift of leaves, transforming them from a dull, dusty beige to a gold so dazzling that I gasp out loud, my rhythm jarred for an instant. I turn another corner and the smell of someone's dinner hangs in the air—something teasingly exotic, with a touch of curry. I take a few sips of water to quiet my taste buds and power on. Presence, I've come to learn, is much more entertaining than distraction.

Despite my whining about it, running has become a close second to gardening in my "peace of mind" ingredient list. It took me close to a year to work up to high intensity cardio sessions most days of the week, as recommended by Dr. Furth at Georgetown Lombardi Comprehensive Cancer Center. As well as reducing my risk of breast cancer recurrence (a very effective fear-based motivation), running—along with boot camp and cardio dance classes sprinkled into my fitness mix—has evolved into an essential pillar of my mindfulness practice.

I learned why running made me feel so good when I read *Spark: The Revolutionary New Science of Exercise and the Brain,* by John J. Ratey, MD.[15] Ratey explains in layman's terms how aerobic exercise triggers chemical reactions in the brain that influence an astounding range of functions. He's not even talking about the "runner's high" that some marathoners experience (I have no intention of ever running long enough to achieve that state).

Research shows that all types of aerobic exercise boost the production of chemicals that reduce stress, anxiety, and depression. This was why running had replaced my decades-long reliance on medication to offset my genetic predisposition to depression. But despite the clear benefits I could recognize on the surface, I was still holding some resentment that cancer was what was "forcing" me to maintain the regimen. Running was still something I felt I "had" to do rather than something I wanted to do.

Ratey's book changed that for me, specifically when he described a class of proteins as being "Miracle-Gro" for the brain. That was language I could understand. The proteins in question, "brain-derived neurotrophic factor" (BDNF), build and maintain brain cell circuitry—the very infrastructure of the brain. As Ratey explains it, BDNF "nourishes neurons like fertilizer," improving their functioning, encouraging growth, and protecting against the process of cell death. In contrast to what most of us learned in school, research over the past decade has proven that we *can* grow new brain cells with the help of BDNF and other protein factors.[16] Aerobic exercise boosts the production of BDNF. Having watched my grandmother sink into severe dementia, unable to recognize me as her granddaughter for the three years I managed her care, I now had yet another reason to lace up my running shoes.

Spark is stuffed with research studies illustrating how cardio exercise staves off or reduces the symptoms of stress, anxiety, depression, ADD/ADHD, hormonal changes, and Alzheimer's, as well as guarding against diabetes, heart disease, stroke, and some forms of cancer.

Confirming what Dr. Furth had already told me, Ratey explained, "Twenty-three of thirty-five studies show an increased risk of breast cancer for those women who are inactive; physically active people have 50 percent less chance of developing colon cancer; and active men over 65 have a 70 percent lower chance of developing the advanced, typically fatal form of prostate cancer."[17]

All forms of aerobic activity have mood-boosting benefits, but you get an even bigger bang for your buck if you combine it with some sort of complex activity that taxes your brain as well. Anything more complicated than walking (running, tennis, kayaking, dancing) goes even further toward strengthening your immune system and improving cognitive performance. And although many aspects of the economist portion of my brain were becoming less pronounced during this stage of my life, I could see that when it came to exercise, the efficiency benefits outweighed the costs by a long shot.

As had been the case with my accidental download of Eckhart Tolle, the universe put Ratey's work in my path just when I needed it most. The monotony of running every day by myself was getting old, and *Spark* (which also cited the benefits of exercising with a buddy or a group) gave me a much-needed motivational jolt. The universe's next gift was a whirling dervish of a man wrapped in sweaty work-out clothes.

The first time I went to Stan's Friday morning cardio dance class (a perfect way to introduce the aerobic exercise plus complex activity that Ratey had recommended), the instructor was talking about a baby who had been born the day before. I assumed Stan was the father. His muscled physique and the jaunty tilt of his baseball cap gave him a youthful air that I didn't question.

I was about to give him a hard time for coming to teach so soon after his baby was born. Then it became clear that Stan wasn't the father, but the grandfather. *Huh?* OK, so when he took his hat off there was no hair underneath. But that's a look for young guys too these days, right?

Before I could give it any more thought, the class began. Stan's broad smile lit up his face and the entire room along with it. He seemed to be infused with the music as he led the first steps that would nudge our heart rates up progressively over the next hour. His energy seeped into my skin, my muscles, even my bones, all of which began to move in sync with Stan.

Music transforms him. Before class, Stan appears to be soft-spoken—a big man with a quiet voice. Most of us are still half-asleep when we shuffle in, and he lets us wake up gently. The instant the playlist starts, however, something kicks in that electrifies his presence. The huge smile triggers upturned lines around his eyes, the mark of a lot of laughing over the years. He twitches his head to the beat while the rest of his body parts move in disparate directions. Following his moves is hard work, so much so that you don't even notice that your heart is pumping at 90 percent of its capacity.

It's a full sensory experience. The visuals are striking—a graceful, muscle-bound man moving as if he were a professional football player and hip-hop dancer combined. And then there's the sweat, which starts to bead on Stan's head by the end of the warm-up. His baseball cap can only absorb so much, though, so he keeps a towel nearby both to dry his head every so often and wipe up the big drops on the floor before we slip.

The sweat is like a living, moving being that connects us all. You see it flying off Stan in front of the group, you feel rivulets of your own sweat sliding down your torso as the class intensifies, and, with enough exertion, you taste the salty fruits of your labor when more sweat streams down your face to the corners of your mouth.

Although the sweat is silent, Stan is not. Hearing him sing along with the music and burst out periodically with a "woo!" or "yeah!" or "that's right!" adds another experiential layer.

I cannot stop smiling. In the early days, I was embarrassed by my lack of smile control. But then I looked around and realized that everyone else was smiling too. I love watching new people in the class struggle to stop grinning. Like me, they always lose the battle. Having felt that tension in myself and watching it in new students, I realize that we are pathetically uncomfortable with unabashed smiling.

I used to think that exercise alone provided the mood boost. But that's not all that's going on in Stan's class. I feel great after I run, but it's not the same as sweating through a session of high-impact dance with Stan. For one thing, the level of concentration needed to follow the steps in the midst of all that's going on at the sensory level requires full presence. One moment of thinking about the past or the future and you've missed Stan's instructions ("turn left!" "knee up!" "hands hips!"), putting you out of sync with the rest of the class. The mirrored walls surrounding us catch every lapse of concentration. There is simply no room for unhelpful thinking to seep in.

On an even higher level, though, it's Stan's inner light and incomparable personal presence that make him such an energizing force. The exercise isn't the only thing lifting my spirits. Stan, himself, generates a contagious joyfulness that I carry home with me after every class. He personifies the power of individuals to improve the world by their positive energy.

I've had some amazing opportunities in recent years to attend talks by leading spiritual teachers—the Dalai Lama, Eckhart Tolle, and Marianne Williamson to name just a few. I've come away from those events feeling an odd combination of deep inner peace and high energy. I've never discussed spiritual issues with Stan. I don't need to. His presence leaves me with that same combination of peace and energy that spiritual giants produce.

A new circle of girlfriends put the finishing touches on my fitness program. A neighbor turned me on to a boot camp group led by two local moms, one of whom I had known for years through soccer. The group was training for a "mud run," which, I came to learn, is an obstacle race course that includes mud pits and other messy challenges. I loved getting dirty in the garden. Why not on the running trail too?

Let me back up here and say that I am an introvert by nature. Though I can be as chatty as the next person, I recharge my batteries by being alone. I've always dealt with painful situations on my own, even to the point of sending Mark to the other side of the hospital room to watch TV during my first several hours of childbirth.

During my cancer treatment and the first year or so of my spiritual awakening process, I retreated even further into my introversion. I was very comfortable being in my own company, and frankly it took a lot less energy than having to explain to other people what I was going through.

Exercise was also a solo venture for me before I joined Stan's class once a week. Running with other people was a hassle, I believed, because it required coordinating schedules. And running while talking was a lot more tiring than running in silence. Why bother?

As soon as I joined Grass Roots Fitness, however, I was hooked. It's all about the energy. Joann and Francine, the owners and class instructors, lead by example. These women are fit, motivated, inspiring moms who never shy away from a challenge. The classes—cardio-strength training, body sculpting, boot camp, and a Body Fusion class that combines tai chi, Pilates, and yoga—not only were effective in strengthening my body, but became an integral part of my social life as well. Each and every woman there was taking charge of her own wellness and emitting positive vibes in the process. Having friends laugh and groan and sweat alongside you, I discovered, transforms work into play.

Classes can be daunting for a lot of people, both from a financial and scheduling standpoint. The good news is, you can get the same benefit for free. All you need to do is grab a friend and head out to the trail together for a walk or run. Just ask the thousand plus women who belong to my town's chapter of Moms Run This Town, a national (and now international) free running group for women. Need a dose of inspiration? Just check out the Vienna/Oakton Moms Run This Town Facebook page, where goals are being set and met on a daily basis with the loudest cheering section you'll ever come across.

Just as I was pondering the motivational power of friends, the universe (using my sister Lisa as the messenger) dropped a new bit of science into my lap:

In a *CBS News* piece on the science of friendship, Dr. James Coan, associate professor of clinical psychology at the University of Virginia, described his lab's research on how and why people with strong circles of friends tend to be healthier and live longer.

Coan's team attached MRI electrode patches to volunteers' heads and told them they'd be zapped at random with mild electrical shocks. The point was to make them nervous, to create "anticipatory anxiety," the same type of uncertainty-based anxiety that most people face in their daily lives. The subjects were put through two series of tests—one round of shocks when they were alone in the room, another while holding the hand of a friend. In every case, the parts of the brain that sense danger were less activated when the friend was there. When the subject was alone, the "danger" areas were on fire. Adding the friend quieted the brain's response to the anticipated danger. Scientists think that translates into lower anxiety levels and reduced pressure on the immune system, which may explain the "good friends leads to better health" phenomenon.[18]

In a lower-tech study, UVA psychology professor Dr. Dennis Proffitt and a team of graduate students asked participants to put on a heavy backpack while standing at the bottom of a hill. Some were alone, others next to a friend. When asked how steep they thought the hill was, those participants who had a friend by their side thought the hill was less steep than those without a friend. The experiment even worked when the person was simply asked to think of a friend—the hill seemed less steep if a friend was in their thoughts, compared to the person left to their own devices. But wait—there's more! Responses even showed that the deeper the friendship and the more time spent with that friend, the less steep the hill became in the view of the participant.[19] Pretty wild.

My Grass Roots girlfriends corroborated this research. Joann convinced me to sign up for a St. Patrick's Day 8K race with her. Having never run more than three miles at a time in my life, it seemed like a huge challenge to increase my distance to almost five miles. But if she was telling me I could do it, maybe I could. Barely recognizing myself, I joined Joann's group of race trainers running up and down the stairwells of a four-story parking garage to increase speed and endurance. She coordinated our running outfits for race day, putting more thought into our fashion choices than I had ever spent on my own wardrobe.

Who knew that shamrock skirts and leprechaun tattoos, combined with almost four thousand other runners on race day, could be so empowering? The collective energy of the crowd congregated in the heart of Washington, D.C., seeped through my skin and lightened my load. I ran those eight kilometers without stopping, Joann by my side and encouraging me every step of the way. As I crossed the finish line, I told her, "Okay. That was fun, but I never need to go any farther than this."

Joann passed the coaching baton to Francine, who somehow convinced me to sign up for a mini-triathlon with her. We didn't know the mud run that the class was doing together was taking place the same weekend as the tri. A few weeks out from the big weekend, I tried to back out of my date with Francine.

"I don't think I can do the tri," I told her. "The mud run's on Saturday, and the tri's on Sunday. I may be too tired, or even injured after the muddy obstacle course. And Jacob's got a soccer game Sunday morning, too. I don't like to miss those games."

Francine looked at me with her big blue eyes. "Really?" was all she said. Like me, she is an experienced mother of teens. Perfectly executed one-word response.

Francine was also doing the mud run the day before. And her son was on Jacob's soccer team. I couldn't use either excuse. Damn.

She reminded me that we'd be finished with the tri before the soccer game even started. It was, after all, a "mini" tri, which is even shorter than a "sprint" tri. With a swim of 250 yards (ten lengths of an indoor pool), four miles on the bike, and only 1.5 miles of running, it's the tapas-plate of triathlons. Suck it up, Martha.

Francine set our training dates. I whined a lot.

"It might rain! Maybe we shouldn't run," I would text Francine the morning of (or sometimes the night before) a scheduled training run.

"See you there," she texted back.

"It's kind of windy. Maybe we shouldn't bike."

"See you there" would pop up on my phone screen.

"I might get wet. Maybe we shouldn't swim."

"See you there."

And she did see me there (most of the time, anyway).

One of my most profound moments of self-awareness happened at the pool, when I realized that I would never be as fast as Francine, who was channeling Michael Phelps in the lane next to me.

"Don't you just want to get it DONE?" Francine asked, when I said I just couldn't get myself to move my arms any faster.

And there was the aha moment . . . I didn't care about getting it over with as fast as possible. I JUST DIDN'T WANT TO SUFFER.

When I told Francine that my desire to not suffer far outweighed my desire to be faster, we laughed about it. But I realized this had become my life's motto.

I didn't care about coming in first. I just wanted to see if I could get myself to the starting line, and hopefully over the finish line. I didn't care if the races I was doing were tiny in comparison to what "real" runners and other athletes did. I didn't care if I finished in the top three (or ten, or one hundred).

Before tackling the triathlon, though, we had the mud run to do. Step one: motivational fashion. Joann and Francine had ordered grass skirts and pink camouflage socks for all of us. The race was sponsored by the U.S. Marine Corps and was being held on a military base, so we fit right in. As had been the case with the St. Patrick's Day run, the crazy outfits had a magic fairy dust effect. We all felt stronger because of it.

It had rained nonstop the day before, turning the entire 3.5-mile course into a slippery, mucky mess. We took off, helping one another along the way, pulling (or pushing) our friends up and over obstacles, sitting down on our butts to slide down slopes that were too slippery to walk on, let alone run. We army-crawled under low-slung barbed wire (which had been replaced by bungee cords), and we ran through the spray of fire hoses. The grass skirts did not fare well.

If I wasn't smiling or laughing, I was on the verge of tears from sheer inspiration. The uniformed Marine volunteers manning the course were motivational without even trying. "Thank you for your service!" we'd shout as we jogged by.

But the image that will stay with me through the end of my days is of the heavyset, white-haired grandmother who, with some help from the crowd, was pulling herself over a ten-foot-high A-frame obstacle when our group arrived. As we cheered her on, she took a breather before descending on the other side, exclaiming, "My husband's a Marine! My son's a Marine! My son-in-law's a Marine! I'm NOT going to quit!"

I didn't quit either, that day or the next. I thought of that grandmother as I dressed for the triathlon at 4:30 the following morning.

My one condition of agreeing to the tri was that Francine promise she wouldn't wait for me once the race started. As a result, she finished first in our 45–49 age group, was the third fastest woman in the race, and the sixteenth fastest competitor, including the men. The lady rocks.

I almost cried when I saw her waiting for me about twenty yards from the finish line, running down the sideline, yelling encouragement, somehow making me run faster just when I was about to curl up in a ball on the ground. Instead, I crossed the line to the announcer's cry: "Congratulations! You're a triathlete!" I waited for him to add "sort of," but it never came.

As had been the case with the mud run, my greatest inspiration that day came from a gray-haired race participant. A sixty-four-year-old woman placed just ahead of me in the race standings. I want to be her when I grow up.

CHAPTER 17

Sound Mind

Meditation. It was the logical next step.

Though my state of mind was calm, clear, and quiet in the garden and during my fitness sessions, I wanted to expand my opportunities to practice presence throughout the rest of my day. Unlike the suburbs and a minivan, meditation had never frightened me. On the contrary, it seemed like a valid instrument to try to offset my negative zigzag energy.

The problem was, I sucked at it.

My sporadic efforts to meditate over the years, drawing primarily on books and CD recordings, were always short-lived and ineffective. Even if I did manage to close myself into my home office and slip on the headphones to listen to a guided meditation on the boom box (before the advent of iPods or smartphones), the slightest distraction—my boys wrestling and knocking over a table lamp, for example—would result in my calling it quits and reverting back to Screaming Martha.

But as I got better at quieting the nasty ego-voice in my head, it occurred to me that I just might be able to bring the peace of mind that I had always had while gardening inside the house with me. Diving further into research on mindfulness, meditation came up again and again as an important addition to my toolbox.

Although the notion of meditation was not off-putting, I didn't fit my own stereotype of the demographic. People I had met over the years who meditated regularly usually had a retreat or two under their belts, were Buddhist, or had lives that weren't dominated by kids, carpools, and overall chaos. I didn't have the time or the interest to escape from my family to spend a week at a meditation retreat. And even after awakening to my spiritual connection with the universe, I have remained denomination-free. Buddhist vows are not in my future.

But the science was too compelling to ignore. A few years ago, the cover of *National Geographic* magazine featured the head of a Buddhist monk covered in electrodes.[20] The article detailed neuroscientists' findings on meditation's impact on health and well-being. Most people are aware, in theory at least, that meditation can help reduce stress and provide an avenue for deeper insight if practiced regularly. Brain scans and other studies of Tibetan monks and western meditators have convinced scientists that the impact extends even further to a healthier immune response, mental health improvements, better decision making, and a happier outlook on life.

But most people still associate meditating with sitting on a mountaintop far removed from the real world, or at least twisted into the lotus position while chanting in an incense-filled sanctuary.

"That's fine for some people," you may have thought, "but I've got real work to do."

My transformation process had convinced me that my work, my purpose, was to deepen my understanding of the power of presence. I wanted to get better at hearing that whisper of wisdom from the universe that came through when I was pulling weeds. Besides, winter was coming. Honing these skills inside the house when I couldn't be in the garden seemed only practical.

Newspaper and magazine articles dropped into my path just when I needed them: "Meditation Gives Brain a Charge" in the *Washington Post*[21] and "How to Get Smarter, One Breath at a Time" in *Time* magazine.[22] The TV news featured Ohio Congressman Tim Ryan spouting the virtues of meditation in his book *A Mindful Nation: How a Simple Practice Can Help Us Reduce Stress, Improve Performance, and Recapture the American Spirit.*[23] And in the least likely of corners, the U.S. Marine Corps was even using mindfulness meditation to treat post-traumatic stress disorder (PTSD) and help soldiers enhance their effectiveness on the field.[24] I didn't need any more convincing. So I headed to the library and checked out a new stack of meditation books. I Googled "how to meditate" and followed the topic on Twitter. I watched Deepak Chopra videos on YouTube. My head was so stuffed with meditation how-to's that I could barely hear myself breathe.

Just as my early forays into running were plagued with physical discomfort, my early attempts at meditating were just as uncomfortable. I would sit cross-legged on a pillow on the floor, trying to keep my back as straight as possible. Within minutes my butt hurt despite the pillow, my hip flexors strained, and my back ached from top to bottom.

As directed by the voice on the guided meditation CD playing in the background, I tried to focus all my attention on my breathing, but the rest of my aches and pains overpowered the narrator. Even if I managed to focus for a couple of minutes, I couldn't maintain an upright posture for very long. I'd allow myself to slump against a wall and would usually end up dozing off.

Despite my failures, everything I was reading about mindfulness practice pointed me toward meditation as a tool that would help strengthen my life skills. "Failure is simply the opportunity to begin again, this time more intelligently," Henry Ford once said.

Remembering the difference that better running gear had made for me, I stocked up on meditation equipment.

First, a timer. After never being sure how long I had been sitting during a meditation session (and being distracted by not knowing), I found an iPhone app that chimed a bell at the beginning and end of whatever length of time I specified. I perused various timer products and chose the Zazen Suite app. Zazen has four different chime options, so you can pick the one that you think a monk on a mountaintop would be ringing for you. I've since come to use the chime not only for unguided meditation sessions, but for every other situation in which monitoring time spent helps me get started and improves my efficiency, from writing, running, and gardening to housecleaning and napping. Ding!

Even more important than the chime, however, is my meditation bench. I had never heard of a meditation bench before, stumbling upon it while searching online for more books on meditation techniques and falling prey to one of those "customers who bought this, also bought this" ads.

The bench works on the same principle as those funky desk chairs you kneel on if you have back problems. You fold your legs under the angled seat, which is about eight inches off the ground and about eighteen inches wide. Your shins rest flat on the floor. The seat distributes the weight comfortably between your hips and shins, with the angle keeping your posture naturally upright with no effort at all. The bench eliminates every ache, every pain. No more excuses. Mine even has hinged legs, so it fits in a tote bag for soccer tournament hotel stays.

Even with so many meditation teachers out there expounding different approaches and techniques, they all agree on three things that *don't* work:

1. Sporadic meditation. Frequency is more important than the length of the session.
2. Beating yourself up when your mind wanders. It's normal that thoughts will continue to come and go.
3. Relying solely on books and other written or recorded sources to learn to meditate.

My earlier attempts at meditation had violated all three of these principles.

The biggest challenge was carving out time every day. Trial and error had taught me that if I didn't finish my meditation before my kids got up, chances were slim that I'd get back to it. So I set my alarm a few minutes earlier than usual, working my way up to longer stretches just as I had done with my running routine.

One question I had was whether running or other full presence-inducing fitness sessions (or even gardening, for that matter) "counted" as meditation. Sakyong Mipham—a Tibetan Lama, meditation master, and marathon runner—wrote a book just for me on this subject. In *Running with the Mind of Meditation: Lessons for Training Body and Mind*, he explained the difference: running trains the body, while meditation trains the mind.[25]

As Dr. Ratey had explained in *Spark*, running strengthens the body and produces chemicals that boost your immune system, decrease stress, and improve brain function. Meditation supports those aspects of physical and mental health as well, with the added benefit of training your mind to help you live more skillfully. A regular meditation practice helps us deal with emotions and life situations; it helps distinguish where various thoughts come from and whether our actions are based on a healthy motivation. Exercise forces presence during the fitness activity, whereas meditation extends presence not only to the time we're sitting in silence, but throughout the day if the mindfulness skills honed during meditation are applied to all our activities and interactions.

Motivation is the starting point for forming any healthy habit. Cancer motivated me to start exercising; the potential for meditation to erase my negative zigzag energy motivated me to commit to a daily practice. I eventually worked up to meditating thirty to forty minutes a day. I thought it still wasn't enough, though, since somewhere I had heard that Deepak Chopra meditates for two or three hours a day, starting at about 3:00 a.m. No thanks.

Forty minutes every morning wasn't sustainable for me. When my schedule got crowded over the holidays and I stayed up later than usual, I would skip meditation if I couldn't rouse myself out of bed early enough to log my time on the bench before the kids got up. Plus, I was still weighed down with worry about whether I was even doing it right. As I tried to stay focused on my breath, all sorts of questions would pop into my head:

Is it okay to split my meditation session between two techniques? For example, focusing on the breath in the first half and watching a candle flame in the second?

If my eyes feel dry when staring at the candle flame, am I allowed to blink?

It said in the book to rest my tongue against my top front teeth and have my lips open a little. But do I breathe through my nose or my mouth?

What happens if my mouth fills up with spit? Am I allowed to swallow?

When (not if) I have a hot flash, am I allowed to adjust my clothes, or is focusing on the pools of sweat collecting behind my knees, under my arms, and running down my sides just an advanced meditation move?

The book says my back should be straight like "a stack of gold coins." Is my back as straight as a stack of gold coins?

Meditation was stressing me out.

I drove two hours to hear the delightful Dalai Lama speak at the University of Virginia. I could have sworn he looked directly at me when he said, "Westerners want their enlightenment fast, and they want it cheap."

Maybe it was time to pay for training. Despite all of my reading and Internet searching, I still felt like I was meditating without a license. But the thought of braving traffic to sit with a bunch of strangers at a meditation center seemed counterproductive and downright inefficient—in other words, the polar opposite of relaxing.

This time the universe came to the rescue through my friend Brian, who lives on the other side of the country but had somehow discovered my blog, which had become my place to air my mindfulness experiments (both the successes and the missteps). Brian sent me the link to a TED talk by mindfulness expert Andy Puddicombe, the title of which was "All It Takes Is 10 Mindful Minutes."[26]

Andy is British, a few years younger than me, with a shaved head and a fit body. Ordained as a Buddhist monk in the Himalayas in his twenties, he served in several countries, gave the robes back after working in the field for eight years, then topped it all off with a degree in circus arts. He insists that being a monk and a circus performer aren't that different—full presence is needed for both.

Andy has made it his life's work to "demystify meditation for the masses," spreading the word through Headspace. com, the organization he cofounded in 2010. All it takes, he says, is ten minutes a day. Andy juggles balls during his TED talk to provide a visual image of how thoughts fly around in our head, making it hard to focus on any one of them when so much content is spinning around in a cramped space.

He makes the case that all you need is a chair and ten minutes a day to achieve calm, clarity, and increased awareness. If you're reading this book, I think it's safe to assume that you have a chair. If you tell me you don't have ten minutes a day to try it, then I'm more convinced than ever that you would benefit from meditation. You don't even need to buy the bench if you don't want to.

Andy's Headspace program appealed to me on the spot. Everyone relates differently to a teacher's style, and there are plenty of other excellent meditation teachers out there. But just as Eckhart Tolle's unique choice of language finally got the spirituality message through to me, as soon as I saw Andy juggling to explain the concept of mindfulness, I knew I had finally found my teacher.

Andy's methodology is based on how easy meditation is. He emphasizes that this is the only time of day when you are not supposed to be "doing" or "creating" anything. You're just stepping back a bit. He doesn't make you feel like a loser if you feel aches or pains or if you are continuously plagued by distraction. "It's normal," he says again and again.

The best part of all is that I could do the program at home, in a hotel room, or any other place of my own choosing, accessing the sessions from my laptop or the Headspace smartphone app. Brilliant! Regular updates of resources on Headspace.com—including clever animations that illustrate the concepts—keep the program fresh, current, and modern-feeling. Andy even does live Q&A sessions on Facebook and Google+. Oh, and he never uses the word "spiritual" or "universe" or any other remotely ethereal terminology. It's the nuts and bolts of mindfulness practice, whether you're a monk or a U.S. Marine.[27] The cost of my yearlong Headspace.com subscription in 2013 worked out to just 26 cents a day.

Here are just a few things I learned:

- Meditation is just as much about other people in your life as it is about you. When you are calmer and happier, you bring out those qualities in others.

- There is no single "correct" technique for meditation. Play around and see what works for you.

- It's normal for thoughts to distract you during your session.

- Meditation teaches you to observe a thought or feeling but not to judge it. You can allow it to be there without identifying with it ("anger" instead of "I am angry"). When it's not tied up with your identity, you don't have to hold on to it.

- Taking things as they come does not mean you shouldn't have hopes and dreams. You can still have a sense of purpose and direction, but absorbing change without resisting it means you go through life with a greater sense of ease.

- As soon as you realize you have strayed into thinking about the past or future, you are back in the present moment (so pat yourself on the back).

- If you fall off the wagon (whether it's your program of meditation, fitness, nutrition, or creative pursuit), just get back on without judging yourself.

- Cultivating gratitude leads to a happy life.
- Change is inevitable—you can deal with it skillfully or unskillfully, depending on your capacity for acceptance.
- Meditation is not about solving problems. It's about living life more skillfully.

Andy summed the whole thing up when he said, "Meditation is about much more than simply watching thoughts go by. It requires an open, interested, and enquiring mind."[28]

What kept me going was realizing with Andy's help that if we approach meditation and life in general from a standpoint of how it will benefit others, we invariably benefit ourselves. As my meditation practice progressed, I became calmer, happier, and more open to those around me. My creative output increased. The tiniest details of life elicited gratitude. And I yelled at my kids a lot less (though parenting will always be the source of my greatest mindfulness failures).

In the back of my mind, I kept thinking, "This would be so much easier to learn if I were at a quiet retreat somewhere." But Andy nixed that. He maintains that it's important to remain in the real world when learning mindfulness and meditation. If we're secluded, we don't see what sets us off. We're not challenged. We can't practice empathy and compassion.

Every moment of our life is experienced through the mind. Every relationship is defined by the experience of our mind. We're taught as tiny children that brushing our teeth should be a daily practice. It seems to me that our minds deserve the same level of dedication and care.

Marianne Williamson—renowned spiritual teacher, best-selling author, and political activist—perhaps summed it up best when she said, "You wouldn't start the day carrying yesterday's dirt on your body. Why would you start your day carrying yesterday's stress in your head?"[29]

Even though I've been meditating daily for about three years as of this writing, some days my sessions are still fraught with an onslaught of runaway thoughts. (Anne Lammott describes this as feeling like a squirrel with shingles.)[30] But most of the time I finish feeling as if I've taken a long, hot bubble bath.

CHAPTER 18

Presence Power

It's one thing to maintain inner calm and clarity when sitting on your meditation bench alone in a quiet room, while your family and most of your neighbors are still asleep. But what about when you're in the trenches of the real world?

As with any process of transformation, the path to living mindfully in the present moment isn't linear. It's two steps forward, one step back, and it requires thousands of reboots along the way.

For me, if it's not my kids triggering a retreat back into the stinky, muddy, fly-ridden swamp of negative reactivity—it's an angry lady at the post office.

One day, just when I thought I was getting the hang of this whole mindfulness thing, I pulled into the parking lot of our local post office. The place was packed, with cars backing out of spaces, cars waiting to get into spaces—simply too many vehicles squeezed onto one confined patch of asphalt. Boxed in, there was nothing to do but be patient while the moving jigsaw puzzle sorted itself out.

A woman pulled up behind me and started honking. Not those polite little "please stop texting—the light is green" honks, but really laying on the horn with full-blown road rage. I laughed out loud and turned to look at the driver. She was attractive, with long dark hair framing big sunglasses, probably in her late thirties or early forties. Maybe she couldn't see far enough ahead to know that what she demanded was impossible.

Nope. She had a perfectly clear view. I laughed at her again, just to be sure she saw me. Once we waited the two excruciatingly long minutes it took to park, we got out of our cars at the same time. I had a vague notion of thinking I should handle the situation with presence, and maybe even compassion. I said in a light tone, "Do you really think that helps?"

"Fuck you!" she said.

"Excuse me?" I replied.

She stated louder this time, "FUCK YOU!"

Again, a little voice was calling out from the distance: *Stay conscious, Martha, be compassionate!*

In a half-assed attempt to comply, I said to her, "Wow, I am so sorry . . . for you."

It had been years since I had exchanged that kind of energy with someone. In my youth—or even ten years ago—I would have jumped at the chance for a slash-and-burn verbal exchange. I used to excel at it. My ego loved taking an opponent down. The worst example of this happened right in front of my young children. We were in a souvenir shop in Luxembourg, paying for a snow globe and a tiny bell. I gave the elderly cashier 50 euros, expecting to get 40 back. But she handed me 10 euros. When I pointed out the error, she claimed I had only given her a 20 euro bill. The exchange heated up, sounding even angrier because we were both speaking German. She accused us of trying to steal from her. I accused her of being too old to do her job properly. The horrified look on my children's faces revealed that their German was better than I realized. Not my proudest moment, to say the least. (We never did get the extra change back, and I'm glad.)

But I thought I had moved a little higher up the personal development curve since that humbling episode.

Although I had told myself I was choosing my words carefully in the post office parking lot, my response was clearly not coming from a place of compassion. I was trying to embarrass the road-rage woman. If the universe passed out report cards, I would have gotten a D at best for how I reacted to that situation.

Her difficulties continued inside the post office, where a dozen customers waited in line. *How is she going to handle this?* I asked myself (not out loud this time).

Sure enough, instead of waiting behind the line painted on the floor a few feet from the counter until it was her turn, she walked right up to the elderly woman who was still being helped and set her purse down next to the customer's elbow. The post office employee just stared neutrally at our angry lady, sensing, perhaps, her short fuse. Postal workers must be trained to disarm disgruntled colleagues and customers alike.

The thing was, I really did feel sorry for her. I remembered what it felt like to be consumed with anger and resentment—the tight feeling in your stomach, tense muscles, clenched jaw, and seething sense of being out-of-control. But I didn't behave in a way that diffused her anger or her pain. Quite the opposite. I reacted to her negativity with my own negative, belittling response, and in doing so brought us both further down. I felt slimy and stinky the rest of the day.

Fast-forward six weeks. It's just a few days before Christmas, and I'm pulling into the very same post office parking lot. I see an open spot between two cars. Nobody is moving, and it's easy to back my van into the space. I use both mirrors and the backup video—all clear.

The ignition clicks off and I start to get out. The door of the car next to me opens and the driver says, "I guess you didn't see me—you almost hit me! You almost ran right into me!" Another angry lady, this one much older than the first.

I was a heartbeat away from getting defensive, but I realized it was my *Groundhog Day* moment. You remember the classic Bill Murray movie, in which his character is forced to relive a particular day over and over again until he gets it right. The universe had given me a second chance.

I almost laughed out loud at the universe's sense of humor. ("Almost" was progress, since my laughing out loud had been the start of the slippery slope during my previous parking lot altercation.)

Mustering my presence, I locked my ego in the closet, took a step back, and said to the woman, "Oh! I'm so sorry!"

But this time I meant it. It wasn't that I believed that I had almost hit her. But I did see real distress in her eyes and feel her fear. I was truly sorry that she was suffering. Empathy trumped defensiveness, and I was able to stay clear-headed.

"Are you alright?" I asked. "What can I do to help? Can I carry your packages for you?"

Disarmed, she grumbled, "I don't have any packages."

Then she hobbled out of her car and started walking very slowly toward the building. She was probably in her late seventies, and physically impaired to boot.

"You're not allowed to rush ahead of me and take my place in line!" she snapped, as I started at my normal walking pace. "The men always do that!"

"How about I just walk next to you? I promise not to get in line in front of you," I said. I slowed to a snail's pace.

"How long have you lived around here?" she asked, in a slightly less grumpy tone.

"Twenty years," I replied.

"I've lived here for fifty years," she said. "We bought our house for $20,000 and now it's worth $750,000."

"Wow!" I said. "Lucky you!"

"Two years ago I went in for routine surgery and the doctor accidentally sliced my bladder open," she said. Our relationship was progressing quickly. "I've never been well since."

Me (again): "I'm so sorry!"

When my ego muttered, *You should tell her you weren't anywhere close to hitting her,* my true self replied, *How important is it, really?*

Inside the building, she had to fill out an envelope. I waited behind her, assuring her I wouldn't take her spot. I ran my fingers along the edges of the package I was sending, staying in tune with my senses.

Fortunately, I wasn't in a huge hurry. As a means to stay present, I focused on my breathing, even counting my inhales and exhales in cycles of ten if I started to feel impatient. Unlike my response to Angry Lady #1, my second chance with Angry Lady #2 showed me that being present could keep me in a nonjudgmental frame of mind. I was able to empathize, which diffused her tension immediately.

I wasn't pandering. I wasn't playing the martyr. I wasn't looking down on her. I wasn't belittling her or myself. I was simply there, paying attention to someone whom most people rushed by. She was frightened and frustrated and lonely, and it sounded as if that was her life experience most of the time (that was probably the case with the cashier in Luxembourg as well).

It was so easy to give her a few minutes of respite. And it felt good to dissolve her negative energy. Presence felt good. It was the exact opposite feeling to the one I had had after my exchange with the f-bomb lady a few weeks earlier. Instead of coming away feeling like a sewer rat, I came away feeling as if I had made the world a little bit brighter.

In the back of my mind, I chuckled at the obvious redo the universe had thrown my way. In what I could only see as a wink in my direction, the woman, after being helped by one post office employee, was redirected to another window—the one where I was being helped. After all my efforts to make sure not to get in front of her in line, she still ended up behind me.

We continued to chat until she finally said, "Do you have time for a cup of coffee?"

I had to pick up Jacob from school and couldn't join her, but we parted with a wave, a smile, and a "Nice to meet you!"

So what had made the difference?

After my demoralizing exchange with Angry Lady #1, I went back to where I started. It had been a few months since I had checked in with Eckhart Tolle, having been focusing instead on the nuts and bolts of meditation. I needed an Eckhart refresher to remind me of the spark that had set off my awakening process. I needed to rejigger my spiritual connectivity.

To be honest, the spiritual stuff still scared me a little, at least in terms of being public about it. I hadn't fully embraced a spiritual identity, which for me evoked either church ladies or the spacey Luna Lovegood (who actually *is* my favorite *Harry Potter* character). In the greater scheme of things, listening to the universe (or Source, or spirit, or God—whatever you choose to call it) was still very new to me. On top of that, my experience didn't feel like "faith," since I wasn't really praying to a separate, external force to help me out. For me, spirituality means feeling my connectedness to the shared consciousness of all of creation. That deeper intelligence helps me live better now, with utmost gratitude and appreciation, during the short blink of time that constitutes my life this time around. I'm not basing my decisions on hoping for something better after I die.

So when I came across mindfulness thought leaders who approached the topic using nonspiritual language, I jumped on that bandwagon. Don't get me wrong—you can practice mindfulness successfully without identifying with the term "spiritual." The science proves it.

But the power of mindfulness and meditation, and the potential for it to change our collective consciousness, I believe, rests in our ability to tap into something deeper, that unseen force that's hard to pin down with one name.

By sweeping the most important piece—our energetic connection with all of creation—under the rug, I wasn't getting the full bang for my buck. Taking the safer, non-spiritual route wasn't enough to overcome my deeper karmic patterns, as evidenced by my bitchy response to Angry Lady #1.

What I had lacked in the post office parking lot the first time was what Eckhart refers to as "presence power." I hadn't had a stored reserve of presence from which to draw in that difficult moment.[31]

Presence power is generated during mindful moments when things are going smoothly. Alertness arises when you take a moment to become mindful, conscious, or meditative. The person subsides and presence comes to the surface. Presence, rather than your personal history, defines you. When you respond to a difficult person with presence and without judgment, you interrupt their cycle of unconscious behavior because you have interrupted your own cycle of unconscious behavior. That's a lot of value added.

Through my meditation practice, I was trying to expand my number of mindful moments each day. Angry Lady #1 showed me that I had only been going through the motions, keeping it on the surface. Without question, lots of things were better. My practice had resulted in less stress, greater clearheadedness, and more creative output compared to my premeditation self.

But the f-bomb lady showed me that when the going gets tough, I need to shift to an even higher level of presence to break my deep-seated, ego-driven habits. I need to fill up on presence power on easy days so that I can draw from it on hard days. I need to step out of the way so that life can steer the situation in a more compassionate direction when my white-knuckled ego is clutching the wheel.

Here are a few opportunities to soak up presence power throughout your day:

- Instead of checking your phone at traffic lights, spend thirty mindful seconds generating presence power.
- Instead of scanning tabloid headlines in grocery store lines, use that time to open up to presence power.

- Instead of turning on the ignition as soon as you sit down in your car, take a brief moment to invite a little presence power.

- Instead of looping your to-do list tape in your head while showering, scrub in some presence power.

- Instead of checking email right up to when your next meeting starts, take a few seconds to breathe in some presence power.

Tiny moments of presence add up to a lot of fuel in your tank when you need to step back from a challenging or stressful situation. Those stored reserves of presence power our capacity for empathy and compassion. And it's only through empathy and compassion (including compassion for ourselves) that we are able to dissolve that negative zigzag energy.

CHAPTER 19
Feng Shui Advanced Moves

Although exercise and meditation led to clear improvements in my personal happiness and well-being, negative chi in our home environment had the potential to undermine my goal of being a net supplier of positive energy in the world.

Two years after my cancer treatment and the kitchen renovation, we tackled what we thought was the remaining major source of bad vibes in the house: the master bathroom. I am a lifelong bath worshiper, retreating for a long hot soak whenever the going gets tough. And when the going is easy. And when the going is somewhere in between. But the peeling 1970s bathtub, moldy grout, and cramped space that constituted the bathroom attached to our bedroom was unmasterful in every respect, not to mention just plain creepy.

As had been the case with meditation, I had reached the limits of my self-taught feng shui skills. Professional guidance would ensure that my bath retreat was designed to maximize happy energy. Enter Feng Shui Master Practitioner Carol Olmstead. Carol's company, Feng Shui for Real Life, provides contemporary, down-to-earth advice to attract positive energy to homes and offices. She's heavy on practicality, light on the woo-woo. A perfect fit for a recovering economist.

Carol approved of our master bath design after making sure that we could not see the toilet from our bedroom. Toilets, in fact, should be as hidden as possible so that energy can't find them and be flushed away. (Our design housed the toilet in a separate commode room. What a relief!)

Plumbing plays a big role in feng shui. As Carol writes in her how-to book *Feng Shui Quick Guide for Home and Office*, leaky faucets "symbolize prosperity, wealth, and abundance dripping down the drain."[32] I could attest to that, given that a leaky faucet in the boys' bathroom had resulted in $900 worth of drywall repair after it had flooded the foyer below. And that was minor in comparison to some of the other floods we had experienced in the house. On the other end of the spectrum, just two weeks after the completion of our kitchen renovation project, a faulty dishwasher spewed water for six hours while we slept, ruining not only the recently installed hardwood floor, but also the entire ceiling and carpet of the newly finished basement below.

My hope was that gutting the master bathroom and replacing all the pipes, faucets, and toilet would protect us from future floods. In the meantime, keeping the rest of the toilet lids down to protect wealth-supporting chi from being flushed away was the least I could do, since I wasn't contributing to family income at the time.

Carol's feng shui methodology clarified three easily identifiable sources of negative chi:

1. things you don't like;
2. things that are broken;
3. things that are cluttered.

Armed with this simple action plan, I went to town with feng shui fixes throughout my home and garden.

Whereas I used to think that the ultimate feng shui decorating scheme was a minimalist landscape with hardly an object in sight, it turns out that possessions are not bad in and of themselves. The important thing is that you really *love* each and every item enough for it to earn a place in your house. Your space should be filled with objects and artwork that elicit joy. Joy injects positive energy into the environment.

On the flip side, if you look at that porcelain cat you inherited from Aunt Betty and think, "Yuck," then you're emitting negative energy into your space. "But I have to keep it because Aunt Betty gave it to me!" you protest. Unless Lord Voldemort taught Aunt Betty how to make Horcruxes, Aunt Betty's soul is not hiding in that dust-collecting cat. If you really love Aunt Betty, consider replacing the ugly cat with a nice photo of her. If you don't have fond, joyful memories of Aunt Betty, you are under no moral obligation to reserve space for her in your home. Sorry, Aunt Betty, but you reap what you sow.

Replacing burned-out light bulbs falls into the "fixing broken things" category of chi management, a quick and easy feng shui cure that brings an instant uptick to my mood. Pay attention to how you feel when you flip on that switch, and you'll see what I mean. Tightening the hinges of sagging doors, fixing stuck drawers, and securing wobbly handrails are all positive chi boosters.

Cleaning out cupboards, closets, and drawers serves to flush out negative chi and makes room for new opportunities, according to feng shui philosophy. Those piles of papers and books on the floor of your office? Flypaper for negative chi. Clearing the clutter from your floors and counters frees pathways for feel-good energy to flow freely.

And then there is the bagua. Although I had read about the bagua—the energy map that assists with feng shui design and placement—it seemed complicated until Carol showed me how easy it is to use. The traditional bagua diagram is shaped like an octagon, but Carol uses a much simpler rectangular grid version.[33]

This contemporary bagua consists of nine evenly sized rectangles labeled with the critical aspects of daily life. By superimposing the chart over your house's floor plan, you can see which areas of your home represent the following areas of your life:

- power/wealth/abundance
- fame/future/reputation
- love/marriage/relationships
- creativity/children/legacy
- compassion/travel/helpful people
- self/career/work
- knowledge/wisdom/harmony
- family/health/community
- well-being/balance

The next step is to choose colors, artwork, and natural elements that support each of the bagua areas according to feng shui principles. The five elements—Fire, Earth, Metal, Water, and Wood—all need to be present in our living and working environments to optimize our well-being. The bagua tells you how to get the most bang for your buck (energetically speaking) in where you place them.

Rather than fully buying into the woo-woo, I used the system as a shortcut since I have neither talent nor patience for home decorating. And I only did the easy, mainstream stuff—no crystals, incense, or altars, which Carol's practical approach doesn't push anyway. But, I reasoned, if my design choices might also help attract happiness, health, wealth, and strong relationships, why not give it a try?

As an example, since our kitchen is located in the fame/future/reputation area of the bagua, I brought in the recommended Fire element via candles and red and orange pots for the houseplants on the windowsill. Jade plants and African Violets symbolize wealth and abundance in feng shui, so I chose those to replace the shriveled cactus that had been there for years. Word has it that spikey, thorny plants cause arguments. Whether it's a placebo effect or not, the new plants soothe me on the spot. The window seat next to these plants is where I do most of my writing, aligning with that whole fame/future/reputation area of my life.

Bedrooms have their own set of prescriptions. Everything in the room should support sleep and your relationship. Pictures of you and your partner are acceptable, but find another place in the house for photos of kids and in-laws. As Carol says, "You wouldn't want them watching you!" Getting the TV out of the bedroom is at the top of the list of feng shui advice, not to mention at the top of every sleep specialist's "How to Sleep Better" list. Feng shui also advises that bedrooms be painted in a skin tone, ranging anywhere from warm beige to pink to any shade of brown, since the goal for most of us is to sleep with a human.

Feng shui principles apply to the outside of the house and yard as well. Dirty windows, cluttered carports and garages, and overgrown plants and shrubs all inhibit the flow of positive chi. I had known this intuitively in the garden for years, feeling an immediate energetic improvement when pruning away dead branches, trimming back ornamental grasses that blocked a stone walkway, or pulling weeds between my perennials. Feng shui gave me a framework to understand the energy I had felt moving through those cleared pathways even before I had the language to talk about it.

Having said that, I remained conservative in my approach. I had no interest in reading the *T'ung Shu* almanac, which has been produced for centuries as a feng shui guide for deciding the best times to move, switch jobs, or even bathe. Nobody is going to tell *me* when it's okay to take a bath. And I had no time for or interest in the highly impractical feng shui cures, although I once came close to carrying out the "Orange Peel Ceremony" to clear bad chi after I had discovered a very muddy son contaminating my previously sparkling soaking tub in my pristine bath retreat. The ceremony would have required me to cover twenty-seven orange segments in hot water and flick the orange-infused liquid all over the room while chanting an affirmation, mantra, or prayer. It was still a bridge too far. The last step of the ceremony, however, is to place fresh flowers in the room, replacing them every three days until you hit day nine, when you can let them stay until they wilt. Now that was right up my alley (though I still didn't do it). I had vowed that I would never delve too far into the impractical side of feng shui. But hadn't I learned by now to never say never?

Despite the fact that I had extended my feng shui plumbing fixes to the rest of the bathrooms by replacing the three other backup-prone toilets in the house, our water woes weren't over.

Mark and Cody were on their way out of town for a weekend-long soccer tournament. Mark made a quick trip to the basement for some provision or another and came up the stairs saying, "Um—the carpet down there is a little wet."

Still in my bathrobe, I bolstered my courage and headed down to the guest bathroom. We hadn't had rain, so any water would need to be coming from the basement plumbing. It was not a good sign that chunks of food and stems of the thyme I had used in the previous night's dinner floated in the shower stall. The sewage system had burped up the garbage disposal detritus, and who knows what else, through the shower drain.

It was a shitty way to start the weekend.

Mark and Cody waved goodbye, and I hunkered down for the cleanup. The plumber was at a loss as to the source of the backup, having not found anything after reaching the end of his snake. And even though it appeared that only a small section of the basement carpet was wet, the plumber informed me that sewage water is rife with unseen microbes that could kill us all.

I soon discovered that sewage water had crept under the wall into the guestroom closet, seeping into cardboard boxes of photographs and the stack of comforters the boys used for sleepovers. Anything wet needed to be chucked.

Digging deep into my new bucket of mindfulness skills, I reminded myself gently: *Take action where you can, Martha, and let go of the rest.*

If I felt stress, anger, or frustration rising, I focused on my breathing, counting my inhalations and exhalations in cycles of ten while I carried load after load of infested items upstairs to the carport. I looked for silver linings and opportunities for gratitude, like insurance paying for a new vanity to replace the ugly, water-logged one that the renters installed after the bathroom had flooded on their watch when we were in Germany. Insurance also covered new carpet in the basement, which would have been fun if I hadn't just replaced it after the kitchen flood.

All in all, I was pretty proud of myself for not freaking out. By staying calm, I was able to conserve my energy for the task at hand, rather than wasting it on drama. Drama is so very exhausting, after all.

I called Carol to tell her about our most recent flood. Although surprised (she knew how diligent I had been about my feng shui plumbing fixes), she had a plausible answer. Sewage backups, according to feng shui, result from the house clearing bad energy out of its system.

I developed my own theory. The sewage backup happened the week before my first colonoscopy. I figured that, by clearing its own bowels, the house was just being empathetic.

Five days later, water poured through the dining-room ceiling, right below that new bathroom of mine.

With no reserves of acceptance or presence power left, I jumped up and down in frustration as water streamed over the edges of my bowl-shaped dining-room light fixture onto the rosewood table and upholstered chairs. This was simply getting eerie.

The bathroom contractor arrived within the hour. Other than a slightly loose faucet cover connection, he couldn't find any problem with the pipes.

"You need a specialist," was all Carol could say once she got over her shock at this latest development. "Something bigger is going on here."

She connected me with Bridget Sarako, CEO of the International Feng Shui Guild and creator of Feng Shui by Bridget. Bridget's website lists her specialties as "On-site and Distant Feng Shui, Dowsing, Space Clearing, Blessings Ceremonies and Zen Attunement© Consultations."[34] Stay with me, people. This was uncharted territory for me too.

In our initial phone consultation, Bridget explained that she could send her energy field down from Saskatchewan, Canada, to check out our little plot of land 1,700 miles away. If she found energetic disturbances that needed fixing, she could take care of that for us.

When I asked about the mechanics of how this all worked, she said she was not a clairvoyant or fortune-teller. Instead of "seeing" what most of us can't, she "feels" the situation by tapping in to the vibration. Then she clears whatever non-beneficial energies she comes across and balances the rest to support the highest good.

Having exhausted all other avenues for an explanation, we were at the end of our rope. So why not? The price was less than what we spend on a new pair of soccer cleats for the boys. I don't buy purses, I don't buy shoes. But I wanted my spiritual dowser and I wanted her now.

Mark, worn out from submitting insurance claim after insurance claim, said simply, "Go for it." Fortunately, he had retired from the CIA by that point, or he may not have been as amenable to my sending a complete stranger a photograph of our house, its inhabitants, our address, the house's floor plan, and a diagram of our property.

It was pretty awkward talking to the boys about it. I would have kept it to myself, but Bridget needed permission from everyone in the family since she'd be checking out all of our chi.

"Can you see under their clothes?" I asked her.

"No, just getting a read on their energy," she reassured me.

"Why do I need to ask them? I don't get their permission before getting them vaccinated," I pointed out.

"It's just my policy. I don't want there to be any privacy concerns," Bridget explained.

Never have I seen such eye-rolling when I brought it up at dinner.

"Are you doing it, Dad?" Jacob asked.

"Yes," Mark said. "It's something Mom wants to do. There's no harm in it."

"Fine," Cody said. "Just don't tell any of my friends."

We had a deal. But they clearly thought I was a whack job.

Bridget was unobtrusive during her visit. I might not even have known that she was there had it not been written on my calendar. She called after her session to brief me on her findings.

It turns out that all sorts of nonbeneficial energies were stuck on our property. Some had to do with geopathic stress, some were related to electromagnetic fields (so-called Curry Lines and Hartman Lines), and some were from interference caused by cellphone towers.

But the water problems—the reason Bridget was on the case—appeared to her as being caused by very old emotional trauma of the land. You heard me. Emotional trauma of the land was making my house cry.

Whatever the trauma was, it probably had something to do with the four curses, four Earth Karma sources (stemming from the curses), and the six or more nonbeneficial energy forms that she encountered in addition to those already listed above.

As Bridget explained it, that last category of nonbeneficials "are sometimes thought of as ghosts, thought forms, or energy beings that are either stuck or move through time."

Okay, then.

Across cultures, and in feng shui specifically, water represents emotions and purification. As she befriended the energies on our property, Bridget was informed that our water incidents stemmed from the land's plea for release and healing.

But what was the source of the trauma in the first place? I asked if my kids' fighting or teen angst could be to blame, but they were off the hook. The trauma had deep historical roots.

Bridget asked me whether anything noteworthy had happened in our local history that might provide a clue.

"Well," I said, "this area had a lot of Civil War action." But I'm no military historian, so I couldn't speculate further.

She suggested that we check my town's website, which confirmed that Vienna had been "an alternate camping ground for the two contending forces" when the Civil War broke out. "This was a confusing time for residents. It was hard to tell friend from foe, and the area changed hands so often that many families moved away for the duration of the war."[35]

Between all that bad blood and violent skirmishes in the neighborhood, trauma was clearly in abundant supply.

What gave both Bridget and me goose bumps, though, was that the first foreign settler within the town limits of Vienna seemed to have been Colonel Charles Broadwater, "a prominent colonial soldier and public servant, who owned much of the land in the region and built his home here in 1754."[36]

Bridget made an immediate connection between our water issues and BroadWATER. "When I get tingly like this," she said, "it tells me we're on to something."

My own goose bumps stemmed from the fact that during our stint in Germany, the senior ranking officer living on our military base was a General Broadwater, whose family did, indeed, stem from the Virginia-based Broadwaters. Was this colonial era Broadwater trying to get a message to me? Maybe, maybe not. The important thing was that Bridget was fixing whatever bad juju had taken root on our property.

Once she had a handle on the source of the water incidents, Bridget explained, she cleared and transformed the nonbeneficial energies, brought in positive healing energy, and balanced everything out to serve the highest good. Not only that, she created an energetic matrix anchored at the four corners of the property to protect us as long as it was needed.

We all feel better after a good cry, especially when we know we've been heard by the target of our outburst. My hope was that now that I was listening to the land and had done what I could to help it heal, we would have fewer insurance claims in our future.

Hiring Bridget took me far beyond my previous comfort zone, making a mockery of my insistence that I would never delve too far into the woo-woo. Whether she really did reach a negotiated settlement with ghosts on my property or not, nothing out of the ordinary has happened since. Okay, we did have one more basement flood a couple of years later after three days of non-stop torrential rain combined with melting snow. But somehow—probably because there was such an obvious cause—it didn't feel creepy. Bridget "visited" once more just to check on things but, unlike her first consultation, she didn't find any unhappy energy lurking about. At least that last incident didn't require an insurance claim, so that was progress.

Today, we have a shiny sump pump installed in the basement. Between Bridget's energy clearing work to improve my land's mental health and the whir of the sump pump when the rain is coming down, I have my bases covered. And it's just sort of fun to feel that the land (and my garden on top of it) knows that I did what I could to heal its negative energy. I guess it's a little like what happened with Angry Lady #2 at the post office on my *Groundhog* day.

As for the rest of my house, though it's still a cycle of order and chaos with varying degrees of inevitable clutter, our feng shui-inspired infrastructure keeps the major pathways for positive chi cleared most of the time. When my head feels cluttered, meditation is the first step. Tidying up the house is the second. Once my internal and external spaces are cleared and positive energy can flow back into those spaces like sunlight, I'm back in my blossoming groove.

CHAPTER 20

Further Wisdom

I used to think suffering put me on a moral high ground. Suffering made me deeper and somehow better, more important than other people.

I used to think that drama made life interesting. The more drama I could stir up, the more interesting my life was and, therefore, the more interesting I was.

I used to think that wonder and adventure could only be found in foreign, exotic places. The further away I was from home, the more alive I was.

I know now that none of that was true.

The garden had tried to tell me this from the earliest days of our relationship, but I had been deaf to her messages. Going back even further, those messages had been right there in the astrology chart reading I had blown off in my youth.

Once my head had quieted ever so slightly during the year of my cancer treatment, I was primed not only to hear, but to understand fully that my frightened ego was behind the false beliefs that defined my sense of self. The realization that I didn't need to buy into every thought that popped into my head brought me instant relief from suffering. For perhaps the first time in my life, I experienced full presence, awareness, and inner peace. All I needed to do was let go of my focus on the past or future and love myself this very moment as I was, where I was. (Easier said than done, of course.)

Letting go of my attachment to suffering and simply saying no to drama engulfed me in calm contentment. I felt as if I had stepped through a door into a new world. Nothing in my external life situation had changed, but I was now able to accept, appreciate, and love every aspect of my existence. I still had no idea what my future entailed, but it didn't matter anymore. I was filled with a sense of purpose.

Externally, it was a solitary experience, since nobody I knew understood what I was going through. My garden was the only one holding my hand the moment I crossed the threshold to awareness. But I soon realized that I wasn't alone at all. Millions of people around the world are awakening to their spiritual connection with the rest of creation, each of them in their own unique way. To reassure me of this, the universe sent a slew of teachers hand-picked just for me. Because that's what the universe does when our hearts are open and our souls are in full bloom. That's what the universe does when we're living in alignment with our purpose. The universe's helping hand is called synchronicity.

What are the chances, for example, of Eckhart Tolle and the Dalai Lama speaking in my area within two weeks of each other, and of my getting to hear *both* of them? Tolle had never visited Washington, D.C., before, but I had been perfectly happy reading his work and watching his talks online. I never would have shelled out for a plane ticket to see him in his home territory of Vancouver, B.C., let alone for one of his international retreats. In a fabulous act of generosity, the universe dropped him into my backyard (well, twenty-five minutes from my backyard). Mark even came with me, providing him a window into my new life perspective. He was struck by how wide-ranging the audience demographic was—a handful of hippie-types here and there, but mostly well-dressed businesspeople.

Although I had been fully satisfied with relying on Tolle's work to guide my nascent spiritual journey (those "other" spiritual teachers were still a little off-putting to me), the universe apparently thought I was ready to broaden my horizons. Out of the blue, within days of my seeing Eckhart Tolle, my brother-in-law surprised me with a ticket to see the head of Tibetan Buddhism speak at the University of Virginia, just two

237

hours from my house. Hearing the delightful Dalai Lama tell the audience that spirituality isn't about religion was just what I needed to hear at that stage of my process; a priceless gift, this time wrapped in a red robe.

Not long after that, I came across Deepak Chopra in an Eckhart Tolle webcast.[37] I had heard of Chopra, and had even watched a few of his meditation lessons online, but he seemed like one of those flashy spiritual celebrities who fell outside of my comfort zone. In the context of his low-key conversation with Eckhart, however, I found I was more open to Chopra's teaching. He explained the causes of human suffering from the perspective of Vedanta, a school of Hindu philosophy that predates Buddha. According to Vedanta, there are five causes of human suffering:

1. not knowing who you are;
2. addiction and craving for permanence in a world that is inherently impermanent;
3. fear of impermanence;
4. identifying with your self-image instead of your self;
5. fear of death, or the unknown.

Chopra pointed out that organized religion capitalizes on number five. Maybe it was because I didn't identify with a specific religion, or maybe it was because I was still young and fortunate enough to live in a safe environment, but fear of what awaits me after I die had never been close to the surface for me. Even when I was on the operating table the day of my mastectomy, my tears stemmed from not having said a proper goodbye to my family rather than fear of where I would end up after death.

Applying Chopra's lesson to my own life, I realized that my suffering stemmed primarily from number one and number four, not knowing my true essence and being too caught up with self-image. As soon as I learned that the ego-based thoughts in my head were not really "me," that my true self was deeper and vaster and so much wiser than that whiny, unhappy, and often bullying ego voice that had controlled me for so long, it was as if a stone had been cleared from above my head, allowing me to soak in the sun's warmth and break through the surface of the soil. With no self-image myth to confine me any longer, I could embrace the realization that being a mother was my most fulfilling and important work at that fleeting juncture of my life. That's not meant to be a blanket statement that all women should be stay-at-home mothers if they are lucky enough to even have that choice. Someone else may be burdened with the opposite self-image scenario—she believes she's expected to be a full-time mother when the universe may have other plans in store for her if she can just muster the courage to dive into the unknown. The point is to listen to the voice of your true, unique self, rather than the fear-mongering that ego stirs up.

Just as I hadn't intentionally gone looking for Eckhart Tolle or Deepak Chopra teachings, I never consciously thought to myself, *Hey, Martha, you should start reading about near-death experiences (NDEs).* But somehow books on the subject started to fall into my path. The story that touched me most deeply was recounted by Anita Moorjani in her memoir *Dying to Be Me: My Journey from Cancer, to Near Death, to True Healing.*[38]

After a grueling, four-year battle with cancer, Moorjani's body finally shut down. Doctors told her family that her organs had failed and she only had a few hours to live. But Moorjani's consciousness was alive and well, able to see what was happening to her while liberated from her broken body. She describes her NDE as a state of pure awareness, with all previously held doctrine and dogma suspended. Like many NDEers, she experienced 360-degree vision and simultaneous perception of all her senses. She saw her life as a tapestry woven through an infinite spectrum of time, in which past, present, and future occurred simultaneously. She could feel, hear, see, and know everything that affected her.

Moorjani was given the choice to stay on the other side or come back. It was a tough decision, since that other realm was pretty great. It would have been easier to stay there, but she felt she had been given a gift of understanding that she had to share.

She was told, "Go back and live your life fearlessly."[39] She then woke up to the shocked faces of her doctors and family members. Her tumors disappeared.

Moorjani has since devoted her life to speaking and writing about the lessons learned from her NDE: "I understood that true joy and happiness could only be found by loving myself, going inward, following my heart, and doing what brought me joy," she wrote.[40] Having witnessed her interconnectedness with all of creation during her NDE, she returned infused with the knowledge that how she feels affects the universe. If she was happy, the universe was happy. If she loved herself, everyone else would love her too. The realization that she was an integral part of the greater whole shifted her perspective away from her previous self-definition, in which she saw herself as a victim who just had things "happen" to her. It became crystal clear to Moorjani that every event—the good and the bad—had been to her benefit and guided her to where she was today.

Moorjani's story reassured me that paying attention to what makes me happy and following that path is not selfish or shallow, as I had previously feared. On the contrary, the universe wants me to be happy. My capacity to make those around me happy—starting with my family and extending out to the rest of the planet—depends on how well I listen to my heart and take purposeful, joy-inspiring action.

Understanding my residual need for credible academic sources, the universe even used brain scientists to show me that rational people were experiencing transformation similar to my own. One of my favorite teachers in this regard is Jill Bolte Taylor, Ph.D., whose book, *My Stroke of Insight: A Brain Scientist's Personal Journey*, inspired a TED talk that has attracted close to eighteen million views.[41]

Bolte Taylor is a Harvard-trained neuroanatomist. In 1996, when she was just thirty-seven years old, she had a stroke that immobilized the entire left side of her brain. As a brain anatomy expert, she was fully aware of what was happening to her as her language center shut down and her sense of boundaries evaporated. Both of those functions operate from the left hemisphere. She wasn't dead, but she experienced the same spiritual revelations reported by Anita Moorjani and many others who had had near-death experiences.

With her brain chatter silenced, Bolte Taylor's memories of her past and dreams for her future evaporated. There was no way around it—the cells that deliberated on past and future were debilitated. The circuitry that told her she was a separate, solid being wasn't functioning. She experienced herself as pure energy and swirling molecules, blending with the eternal flow of all universal energy. "I was no longer isolated and alone. My soul was as big as the universe and frolicked with glee in a boundless sea."[42]

For her entire life, she had been committed to cramming in as much "doing" as she could, as quickly as she could. "On this special day, I learned the meaning of simply 'being.'"[43] And it was beautiful.

Reading about Bolte Taylor's forced shift from "doing" to "being" reminded me of another famous teacher's lesson. The Bible recounts the story of Mary and her sister Martha hosting Jesus when he came for a visit. Mary sat and listened attentively to all that Jesus had to say, while Martha huffed and puffed around the place cooking and cleaning. Martha complained to Jesus that she was left with all the work while Mary sat on her butt. Jesus told Martha to sit down and stop sweating the small stuff.[44]

Even though Bolte Taylor was aware that she couldn't walk or talk, understand language, read or write, or even roll her body over, she knew she was okay. With her intellectual left brain switched off, she became aware that, even with a non-functioning body, she was still "the miraculous power of life." Her ego was knocked unconscious by the stroke, allowing her to perceive herself as perfect, whole, and beautiful just the way she was.

My brief account may suggest that Bolte Taylor's experience was like a magical walk in the park. On the contrary, her recovery entailed a steep, rocky, eight-year-long journey before her left hemisphere functioned fully again.

Some people helped her recovery—her mother at the top of that list, but others didn't. Bolte Taylor and Moorjani (along with many other NDEers) became highly attuned to what others felt. They experienced personally the emotions behind other people's body language and facial expressions. These accounts reminded me of my own heightened sensitivity to other people's energy—including being overly sensitive to others' stress—during my recovery process. Bolte Taylor writes, "I paid very close attention to how energy dynamics affected me. I realized that some people brought me energy while others took it away."[45]

She learned how to feel the physical component of emotion: "Joy was a feeling in my body. Peace was a feeling in my body . . . . I learned I had the power to choose whether to hook into a feeling and prolong its presence in my body, or just let it quickly flow right out of me."[46] In fact, it only takes ninety seconds for the chemicals induced by a negative external trigger to be washed out of our system, she explains, as long as we don't ruminate and effectively retrigger the negative emotion cycle.

Having experienced the bliss of a quiet, nonjudgmental mind in the midst of her stroke, Bolte Taylor consciously chose to keep the circuits responsible for old, painful emotions switched off as she recovered.[47]

Staying connected to our right brain is key to inner peace, plain and simple. Bolte Taylor describes our right hemisphere consciousness as "completely committed to the expression of peace, love, joy, and compassion in the world."[48] The right brain sees the richness of the present moment and is filled with gratitude for every aspect of life. The right brain is eternally optimistic, doesn't judge things as good or bad, right or wrong. Everyone is equal in the eyes of the right brain.

She sums up her right brain as being "the seat of my divine mind, the knower, the wise woman, and the observer. It is my intuition and higher consciousness."[49]

But don't throw out the whole left brain like a baby with the bathwater. It's true that the left hemisphere character can be mean, arrogant, and verbally abusive. It can worry incessantly and be stubborn, sarcastic, and/or jealous (the ego center lives there, remember?). But Bolte Taylor shows us that we can consciously choose which parts of our left brain to use, and which parts to keep switched off.

The early days of my spiritual awakening process were a much milder version of Bolte Taylor's stroke experience. I had taken up residence in my right brain and didn't want to budge. My ego voice was silent. I was living fully in the present moment (Mark was there to remind me when the boys had soccer practice). And I basked in the flow of universal energy that I sensed all around me—especially in the garden.

Although it was a nice respite from the real world, it wasn't sustainable.

Because what's the point of awakening to our spirituality if we're not going to do something purposeful with this precious understanding? The universe wants us to create, to make the world a better place, to express itself through each of us as we follow our passions.

My left brain gets things done. It keeps me disciplined and on a schedule. It writes my to-do lists, nudges me out of bed in the morning to meditate, maintains my fitness program, puts dinner on the table, gets this book written. My left brain is the tool I use to communicate with the external world.

While my right brain is the source of creativity, I need my left brain to translate ideas into action. My right brain feels the energy flowing around and through me, but my left brain does the hard work of clearing clutter to improve pathways for positive chi. It's taken me a couple of years to learn to appreciate the productive parts of my left brain after being held hostage for so long by the relatively tiny, fearful, and unhelpful ego portion that resides there.

All of the teachers I've discussed here and many more along the way have strengthened my ability to observe my thoughts in an open, nonjudgmental, and loving fashion—just as the universe observes all of humanity. Meditation and other presence-inducing mindfulness practices have taught me to love and appreciate each and every part of myself and, since we are all connected, each and every part of us all.

CHAPTER 21

In Bloom

P lants teach us that brains may be just a little overrated.
A rebel group of plant scientists interviewed by
Michael Pollan for his *New Yorker* piece on intelligent plants
argues that plants are able to think and learn just as well, if
not better, than animals.[50] Instead of brains (which would be
impractical for plants since they can't run away from pred-
ators to protect internal organs), plants have electrical and
chemical signaling systems that act like our nervous systems.
If our brains are eaten, that's it. Plants, in contrast, can lose
up to 90 percent of their above-ground bodies without dying.

We think we're at the top of the planet's hierarchy because
we have these big beautiful brains. But plants comprise 99
percent of the earth's biomass. If a village or town or even a
single house is abandoned by humans—heck, even if we just
go on vacation for two weeks—plants move in and take over.
Plants do just fine without us, but humans and animals can't

survive without plants. Plants take "resilience" to a new level. Who in the animal kingdom can make food out of light, after all? But because the lives of plants unfold in a much slower dimension of time, we tend to underestimate them.

Plants know that we're all connected. Suzanne Simard, a forest ecologist at the University of British Columbia and one of the scientists interviewed for Pollan's article, has shown that trees in a forest organize themselves into networks using an invisible underground web of fungi that connects their roots. They use the network—which researchers have dubbed "the wood-wide web"—to warn each other of insect attacks and distribute carbon, nitrogen, and water to trees in need.

Simard's research group injected fir trees with radioactive carbon isotopes, then tracked the isotopes' movement through the forest community using several sensing methods, including a Geiger counter. Within days, radioactive carbon had been transferred from tree to tree. Every tree in a thirty meters square plot was connected to the network. The oldest trees functioned as hubs, with some showing as many as forty-seven connections—the forest equivalent of Chicago's O'Hare International Airport.

"Mother trees," the connection pattern showed, use the network to send nutrients to shaded seedlings, including their offspring—which the trees apparently recognize as kin—until they're tall enough to reach their own light source. Cooperation was even observed between different species of trees.

The cooperative wood-wide web results in a healthier forest community, more photosynthesis, and greater resilience in the face of disturbance. Look how much better things run when human ego isn't mucking things up.

Pollan concludes that the "brainlessness" of plants "turns out to be their strength, and perhaps the most valuable inspiration we can take from them."[51]

Although scientists argue over the semantics (some react quite vehemently to the notion that plants have "intelligence" or can "learn"), nobody seems to be questioning the data itself. And since they can't understand it, the old guard rejects the "smart plant" label. But there seems to be no getting around the research results. As one scientist featured in Pollan's article said, "There is some unifying mechanism across living systems that can process information and learn."[52]

That "unifying mechanism across living systems" is what my garden introduced me to twenty years ago. It's the magic I sense whenever I'm in the midst of nature. It's the magic to which mindfulness connects me when I'm in the present moment.

In 1911, Frances Hodgson Burnett wrote *The Secret Garden*.[53] The book was one of my favorites as a child, with the mystery and transformative power of gardens blossoming through each and every page. Decades after my first reading, synchronicity pulled me to a sumptuous lavender leather-bound copy on the Barnes and Noble sale rack. Although I had remembered the overarching themes of the restorative power of nature, nurturing a piece of earth, and friendship, rereading it all these years later led me to gasp at the parallels with my spiritual awakening process.

I remembered that Mary, the main character who had been sent to live with her uncle after her parents died, started out as a sickly, miserable brat of a girl. I remembered Dickon, the gentle Yorkshire boy who communed with animals and introduced Mary to the power of nature. I remembered Colin, the crippled cousin whom Mary and Dickon brought to the secret garden where he was healed. But the adult characters had faded from my memory. It was Mary's uncle (Colin's father) who caught my attention this time around.

Archibald Craven traveled frequently, attempting to escape his grief over the death of his wife a decade earlier. But one day, after walking for hours in Austria's Tyrol, he lay down for a nap by a stream. He heard the babble of the water, saw the birds come to drink from it. "It seemed like a thing alive and yet its tiny voice made the stillness seem deeper." He fell into a trance-like state that brought every tiny detail into focus—sunlight bouncing off the surface of the stream, wet leaves of blue forget-me-nots growing at the water's edge.

"It was as if a sweet clear spring had begun to rise in a stagnant pool and had risen and risen until at last it swept the dark water away."[54]

This was exactly the feeling I had had that day in the garden when I recognized that the ego voice in my head wasn't "me." Once I cleared the pathway for my true self to rise to the surface and shed light on my connectedness with the rest of creation, I felt released. For the first time, I understood that my entire life was infused with meaning, that I was an essential part of the universe.

For those of us who can't skip away to Austria, or to an ashram in India, or to any other type of official spiritual retreat that costs both money and time, a garden is a pretty good stand-in. Gardens trigger our senses, pull us into the present moment, evoke wonder and magic, blanket us in beauty, and connect us with unseen forces (including that wood-wide web beneath our feet).

I've gotten to the point in my life where I don't need to understand exactly how, why, or when those unseen forces operate. It's a lot more fun to play with crazy possibilities, to be open to the magic. I'll go with what Anita Moorjani learned from her near-death experience: "My sense is that the very act of needing certainty is a hindrance to experiencing greater levels of awareness."[55]

No matter how many teachers I follow, no matter how many books I read, the garden has always offered up the same lessons. It has taught me to be patient, to let go of the need to control, to let go of expectations. The garden is a place of and for transformation. Most importantly, the garden taught me that a quiet mind is a calm, content, and aware mind, open to hearing the messages whispered from the universe to our hearts. And from that place, our sense of purpose arises.

A famous Zen proverb says, "Before enlightenment chop wood, carry water. After enlightenment chop wood, carry water." (Some translations use "awakening" instead of "enlightenment.") It means that spiritually awakened living still entails the mundane tasks of daily life, but that we bring new eyes and fresh awareness to the work.

Clearing dead wood and weeds, carrying water to new plantings, plunging my trowel into the earth to bury seeds or root balls—these activities brought me to my senses, and therefore to presence, long before I understood the broader power of mindfulness. The garden introduced me to the magic, but it took me years to find that same level of peace inside my home. I was too busy and stressed to invite it in.

Before awakening, my equivalent of chopping wood and carrying water was folding laundry, doing dishes, and driving carpools, all of which made me feel resentful as long as my ego was at the steering wheel. Once I pulled the curtain away and saw that it was merely a tiny, insubstantial part of my brain that was generating fear-based thoughts and not my true self, resistance and resentment dissolved.

Cancer set the stage for a massive reorientation, forcing me to clear my calendar, say no to unfulfilling work, and turn my attention inward. I learned to breathe and feel the energy around me, first through the garden, then through meditation, then through simple acts of cultivating mindful moments throughout the day. I learned that external order nurtures internal order. I learned that less is more.

Fewer distractions helped to quiet the chatter in my head, allowing purposeful messages to rise to the surface from time to time, one of the most important being that the nature of my own energy is contagious to those around me. I learned to filter the thoughts that serve me from those that hold me back. And I learned to look for space *between* the thoughts, during which I can bask in the calming peace of stillness if only for a nanosecond. Sometimes nanoseconds are enough to rein in a reaction that we'll later regret.

A garden, of course, isn't the only portal to inner stillness. Any activity that brings you to your senses, and therefore into the present moment, can serve the same purpose. For my son, it's fishing. For my sister, it's horseback riding. For others it's running, hiking, yoga, painting, cooking, photography, or simply walking in the woods. War veterans suffering from PTSD are discovering that the deep quiet experienced during scuba diving muffles their nightmares of the past and anchors them in the beauty of the present moment. Becoming familiar with that feeling of present stillness is the cornerstone of mindfulness. Meditation broadens and deepens the practice. I use the word "practice" because mindfulness training is never finished. It's a skill to be honed over a lifetime.

People ask me if I am a Buddhist since I meditate and have a present-moment focus. I'm as much a Buddhist as I am a Christian, Jew, Muslim, Hindu, or any of the other man-made rule sets. All these religious structures originated from the same spiritual truth, expressed through different cultural and historical frameworks. And many people, of course, have discovered true inner peace and enlightenment within the structure of organized religions. But ego loves to wreak havoc when there's an opportunity to pit people against each other. In my view, religions have been highly susceptible to those shenanigans. And once ego elbows its way in, suffering follows on its heels.

I don't believe that our limited human brains will ever be able to understand the workings of the universe enough to identify "the one and only truth." I pick and choose from teachings cafeteria-style, but I'm more apt to tap into my own heart's guidance. Rules make many people feel safe, but when it comes to connecting with the universe, I feel rules confine me. And although the sense of community offered by religious congregations is appealing, my personal cost-benefit analysis tips the scales in favor of independence. Besides, I like having my Sundays free for soccer games.

So I stay open to both old and new stuff. I don't check my horoscope (I like to be surprised), but I did venture into a New Age store to buy four rose quartz crystals to plant in the corners of my garden. Bridget, my Saskatchewan-based feng shui spiritual dowser, prescribed rose quartz to anchor my property in love. While I was at it, I bought a little chunk of green calcite, which the store owner suggested for diffusing teenage emotional stress in the house. It can't hurt. Plus, it's fun to experiment with the universe's creativity. But I made sure the neighbors didn't see me walking my property line and planting those pieces of pink stone.

In the end, it all comes back to finding stillness and staying present in the midst of a chaotic world. The goal is not to be "happy" all the time. Happy is great, but it's only one aspect of the ebb and flow of normal human emotions. Living mindfully, with intention and purpose in the present moment, results in a sense of steady, confident, contented joy.

Mindfulness isn't about papering our walls with inspirational quotes and repeating positive thoughts to ourselves. It's about following our passion and engaging in action that inspires and brings out the best in us. This is "being" action, rather than "doing" action.

Shit still happens, no doubt about it. Emotional pain is part of the human experience. It's how we react to life's challenging moments that minimizes our net suffering. Do we take action where we can and let go of the rest, or do we continue to churn up negative emotions, stress, and anxiety by resisting what we can't undo?

Although we often lose sight of it, especially during our darkest times, calm is always accessible in the background. Andy Puddicombe uses the analogy of blue sky always being there, even on cloudy days.[56] If we follow Jill Bolte Taylor's advice to "step to the right" brain, we can tap into our connection with all of creation and thereby experience peace.

My garden always has something to say on these matters. As part of a challenge I undertook in 2014 to take a photo every day of the year and post it on the 365project.org website, I focused my camera lens on a forsythia bud. It had been a long, drawn out winter, and I was determined to will the arrival of spring by focusing all my energy on that little wrapped up package, photographing the bud every day until it bloomed.

My guess was that it would take three or four photo shoots. It took fifteen. Here's what I learned:

1. Nature always moves forward.
2. Noticing the details makes the journey richer.
3. Celebrate tiny progress.
4. Go at your own pace, without trying to please others.
5. Expect setbacks.
6. Practice acceptance and nonresistance.
7. Action isn't everything.
8. Some days will be boring.
9. Rainy days can make things sparkle.
10. Some days you will question the universe's intention.

11. Some days you will lose your compass.

12. Tiny bits of progress each day add up to something big.

13. Sometimes you just need to take a step back.

14. Don't get distracted by what the other buds are doing.

15. Find joy in every stage of the bloom, rather than focusing on when it will be "finished."

I learned many other lessons during that year-long photography challenge, first and foremost the importance of answering the call of inspiration. It was the same year I had committed to writing this book, and I was reluctant to embark on two major creative challenges at once. But I approached the photography project as a mindfulness exercise, an opportunity to stop for a few minutes every day to rest my attention on something beautiful, or at least interesting (for me those two words are almost interchangable). Once my garden came into bloom that spring, I had discovered my niche. My photographs evolved into their own meditations, celebrating the wonder of nature's tiniest details. Yet another gift from my garden.

Here's what mindfulness has come to look like for me:

I stand in front of the sink in the morning after the kids have left for school, overwhelmed by piles of dirty dishes. Usually Mark or the boys do them after dinner, but soccer practice, homework, and tax season must have gotten in the way the night before.

There was a time when I would have been furious to wake up to find dishes still in the sink. But furious doesn't feel good anymore and I accept the reality of the situation. The dishes need to be done, and there is no reason I can't do them. The ego voice in my head makes a weak attempt with *But . . . but . . . this deserves some drama, doesn't it?* I tell it to be quiet and start to untangle the pots from the dishes.

The Today Show might take my mind off the drudgery of dish washing, but then I think better of it. Instead, I will use the opportunity to practice presence.

Rinsing the white plates, my thoughts turn to my mother, who told me when Mark and I were choosing our wedding-gift registry items that white would go with anything. She was right, even before knowing that I would develop a tablecloth fetish later in life that would compete with trendy plate colors. I feel grateful that my practical mother is not only alive and well, but such an integral part of my sons' lives, not to mention my biggest cheerleader.

If the TV had been on, I wouldn't have had the spacious-ness in my head to allow those memories and epiphanies to breeze through, like the cherry blossoms floating off the tree outside my kitchen window.

I turn to look at the cherry tree, and it is astonishing. I thought it was at its peak a week ago and, indeed, a pink carpet is spread around its base. But the branches are still heavy with blossoms, filling the view outside our upstairs and downstairs windows. The cells in my own body hum. A couple of minutes of tree gazing pass, interrupting the dishes. That's okay. I am no longer overscheduled.

Back to the dishes. A woodpecker hammers somewhere in the distance, which I wouldn't have heard if Matt Lauer had been interviewing some random celebrity in the background.

I glance over my shoulder again to make sure the bird feeders are full. I am struck by how good the yard looks despite the fact that it is April and I have done none of the usual winter cleanup and pruning. I normally start in late February, but the bathroom renovation project kept me inside, and I had yet to get organized with outside work. The thing is, once I start in the garden, I cannot stop. Grocery shopping doesn't get done, laundry piles up, dinners fall by the wayside. My gardening overalls are embarrassing to teenagers, so I have to change clothes for carpool driving. I know these things, and since I cannot do "only a little" gardening, I have done none at all.

But to my relief, I see that the countless hours I have spent in all the previous years of gardening this small plot of land have paid off. The foundation is set. The soil is good. The plant choices were right, and when they weren't, they were yanked out and replaced with a better choice. Yes, weeds are taking over the gaps in the beds, but I let go of it for the time being. I focus instead on the saucy patches of color flaunted by the daffodils, tulips, and my favorite fritillaria.

I can't help myself. I grab some scissors and a tiny vase, then venture outside in my slippers to rescue a few treasures from the weed war frontlines. The purple fritillaria, tulip-shaped but hanging like church bells, have plum-colored, checkered petals. That's right—checkered. Or maybe it's more of a snakeskin pattern. Either way it's one of the wackiest flowers you'll ever come across. To give the fritillaria some company, I snip a sprig each of variegated false solomon seal and lime-green euphorbia, providing a glowing backdrop for the otherworldly fritillaria.

But it is cold outside, and the dishes are calling. I set the vase of flowers by the sink and get back to washing. I resist the urge to check email. The flowers are better than Facebook or TV. I finish the dishes and feel happy.

I still yell from time to time. Living with teenagers is the ultimate mindfulness practice. You get to try over and over and over again to stay present. I fail about 40 percent of the time, but that's a big improvement from my zigzag mama days.

Rather than berate myself about it, I remember that even the Dalai Lama gets mad sometimes. I heard him say so myself. That peanut-sized fight-or-flight area of our brains can still be poked in all of us, even in the leader of Tibetan Buddhism. But he steps back and lets those feelings flow out of him without holding onto the negative emotion. I try to do the same. If Jill Bolte Taylor is right, that should only take about ninety seconds.

Stepping back gets easier with practice, especially if you ask yourself, "How important is this thing that's making me mad, anyway?" With a little perspective after taking a breath, problems become mere situations. Take action on your situation and then allow life to play out. Continued questioning and resistance is just energy-sapping mental noise. The better I get at allowing life to happen, at taking mindful action where I can but then stepping back and not resisting what I can't control, the faster things fall into place for me.

We all have the power to increase the supply of joy in our lives. If we care for our bodies, train our minds to recognize which thoughts serve our highest purpose and which thoughts we should ignore, and embrace our connectedness with the rest of creation, our individual and collective quality of life will improve significantly.

Thanks so much for listening, both to my story and, much more importantly, to your heart, where the seeds of joy are buried and waiting for your help to see the light of day.

Acknowledgments

So many people had a part in helping this book come into bloom. My mother, Ellen Van Buren, planted the seed with her gift of *The Memoir Project: A Thoroughly Non-Standardized Text for Writing and Life*, by Marion Roach Smith. I can't think of a braver deed than giving your child a book on memoir writing. My equally brave sisters Lisa Cohen and Sue Rolen added their voices to my mother's cheerleading efforts. I love you all and wouldn't have had the courage to move forward without your support and encouragement.

Marion Roach Smith not only wrote the book that taught me to write with intention, she eventually became my book coach, guiding my decisions on which of my personal stories provided fertilizer and which were weeds that impeded the narrative's growth. Her sister Margaret Roach—gifted author, renowned organic gardener, blogger at awaytogarden.com, and marketing whiz who used to work for that "other" Martha—helped to cultivate my website and marketing platform. My deepest thanks go out to these two wise, delightful women.

Nobody is luckier than I when it comes to having a rich garden of smart, talented friends upon whom to call for help. My writing group girlfriends Katherine Hutt and Laura Bligh provided much needed support when I was trying to get traction on the story. Alice Slayton Clark, Yoon Park, Felice Apter, Lauren Crum, and Patrick Scott were kind enough to provide thoughtful comments on the first completed draft, which guided my subsequent revisions (of which there were many). Nick Madigan, Kathleen Caruso, Sarah McDougall, Mary Beth Kelly, and Cody Gardiner comprised my copyediting and proofreading team, the gardener's equivalent of deadheading. "Thank you" doesn't go nearly far enough to express my gratitude.

I am especially appreciative of the help of two friends who went above and beyond, reviewing multiple drafts, encouraging me to go deeper and do better. Marcia Greenberg, your detailed comments (including on revisions) reflected not only your law school and college professor experience, but also our twenty-five years of friendship. Thank you for caring so deeply.

Bill Apablasa, you should have been included in the teachers mentioned in Chapter 20: Further Wisdom. Discovering your work at TheOther999Rooms.com was among the greatest examples of synchronicity in my journey. Thank you for showing me how to write about mindfulness and conscious living with humor and lightness. And thank you, as well, for the countless hours you spent reading draft after draft of this book. Your repeated admonition of "It needs more Martha" pushed me to work harder and trust my own voice. Many thanks to the folks at 1106 Design for designing my cover and interior layout. My dear friend Doris Ličan Milošević, having offered to help with any other creative work I might need, designed my beautiful website logo and other marketing materials from her perch in Singapore. Tara DuBois of Unbound Website Creations took all the moving parts and built http://www.marthabrettschneider.com into a garden where my creative work can flourish.

I wouldn't have been able to write this book without the support of my circle of fitness mentors and friends: Joann Edwards Meginley and Francine Vitek of Grass Roots Fitness, Stan Stewart at Anytime Fitness of Vienna, and the amazing group of women who make up the Vienna/Oakton, Virginia, chapter of Moms Run This Town. Book writing is a solitary activity that has driven some people quite mad. You gave me a reason to get out of the house and out of my head, helped recharge my batteries, and provided the inspiration I needed to just keep going. Thank you for all of that, as well as allowing me to include you in my story.

Carol Olmstead and Bridget Saraka, thank you for helping me clear pathways for positive energy to flow into my home environment, which supported both my personal growth and my writing, and for your permission to share our adventures in this book.

My deepest gratitude, of course, goes to the three most important people in my life—my husband, Mark Gardiner, and our sons, Cody and Jacob. It's hard enough being the kid whose mother has breast cancer. Being the kid whose mother then shares her (and their) story—even the weird parts—with the world requires even more courage. Thank you for your permission, your support, your love. Cody and Jacob, you are my inspiration, my most important teachers, my greatest gift to the world. And Mark, thank you for your patience, love, and devotion, even as I evolved into a very different person from the one you married. I love you more than I will ever be able to express.

Notes

1. http://www.invasivespecies.wa.gov/priorities/snakehead.shtml.
2. http://www.dcr.virginia.gov/natural_heritage/invspinfo.shtml.
3. Michael Pollan, "The Intelligent Plant," *The New Yorker,* December 16, 2013, http://www.newyorker.com/ magazine/2013/12/23/the-intelligent-plant.
4. Our local elementary school finally switched from half-day to full-day kindergarten in 2013.
5. Gill Hale, Stella Martin, and Josephine De Winter, *Feng Shui Your Life: Enhancing Energies for Home and Spirit* (London: Southwater, 2007), 58.
6. Freecycle.org's mission as stated on its website is: "To build a worldwide gifting movement that reduces waste, saves precious resources & eases the burden on our landfills while enabling our members to benefit from the strength of a larger community" http://www.freecycle.org.
7. Federal Women's Health and Cancer Rights Act of 1988, http://www.cancer.org/treatment/ findingandpayingfortreatment/managinginsuranceissues/ womens-health-and-cancer-rights-act.
8. http://www.cancer.gov/about-cancer/causes-prevention/risk/ alcohol/alcoholfact-sheet.
9. Eckhart Tolle, *A New Earth: Awakening to Your Life's Purpose* (New York: Plume, 2006).

10. Ibid., 10.

11. Ibid., 13–15.

12. Including Eckhart Tolle's international bestseller *The Power of Now: A Guide to Spiritual Enlightenment* (Novato: New World Library, 1999).

13. Jon Kabat-Zinn, founder of the Mindfulness-Based Stress Reduction Program at the University of Massachusetts Medical School, defines mindfulness this way: "Mindfulness means paying attention in a particular way; on purpose, in the present moment, and non-judgmentally" (http://www.umassmed.edu/cfm/About-Us/people/2-Meet-Our-Faculty/Kabat-Zinn-Profile/).

14. Bette Midler founded the New York Restoration Project (NYRP) in 1995 to preserve community gardens and other green spaces in New York City (http://www.nyrp.org).

15. John J. Ratey, MD with Eric Hagerman, *Spark: The Revolutionary New Science of Exercise and the Brain* (New York: Little, Brown and Company, 2008).

16. Ibid., 38–40.

17. Ibid., 84.

18. "Friendship: Close Ties That Enhance, Extend Life," CBS News, March 17, 2013, http://www.cbsnews.com/news/friendship-close-ties-that-enhance-extend-life/.

19. Ibid.

20. http://science.nationalgeographic.com/science/health-and-human-body/humanbody/mind-brain/.

21. Marc Kaufmann, "Meditation Gives Brain a Charge, Study Finds," *Washington Post,* Jan. 3, 2005, http://www.washingtonpost.com/wp-dyn/articles/A43006-2005Jan2.html.

22. Lisa Cullen, "How to Get Smarter, One Breath at a Time," *Time,* January 10, 2006, http://content.time.com/time/magazine/article/0,9171,1147167,00.html.

23. Tim Ryan, *A Mindful Nation: How a Simple Practice Can Help Us Reduce Stress, Improve Performance, and Recapture the American Spirit* (New York: Hay House, 2012).

24. David Kohn, "Mindfulness and Meditation Training Could Ease PTSD Symptoms, Researchers Say," *Washington Post,* February 18, 2013, https://www.washingtonpost.com/national/health-science/mindfulness-and-meditationtraining-could-ease-ptsd-symptoms-researchers-say/2013/02/16/a296a52a-4ad2-11e2-b709-667035ff9029_story.html.

25. Sakyong Mipham, *Running with the Mind of Meditation: Lessons for Training Body and Mind* (New York: Three Rivers Press, 2012).

26. Andy Puddicombe, "All It Takes Is 10 Mindful Minutes," TEDSalon London, filmed November 2012, http://www.ted.com/talks/andy_puddicombe_all_it_takes_is_10_mindful_minutes.

27. This is not a paid advertisement for Headspace. Many other effective meditation programs are on the market as well. Do your research and find the teacher who speaks to you. For me, it was a juggling ex-monk.

28. http://www.headspace.com.

29. Marianne Williamson, "The Law of Divine Compensation" (lecture, Unity of Washington, D.C., November 30, 2012, New York: HarperCollins, 2012).

30. https://www.facebook.com/AnneLamott/posts/742785572517755.

31. "Presence Power," August 1, 2010, http://www.eckharttolletv.com.

32. Carol M. Olmstead, *Feng Shui Quick Guide for Home and Office: Secrets for Attracting Wealth, Harmony, and Love* (Santa Fe: Feng Shui Multimedia, 2009), 162.

33. For more on feng shui basics, check out Carol's website at http://fengshuiforreallife.com/about/Feng_Shui_basics/index.html.

34. http://fengshuibybridget.com.

35. http://www.viennava.gov/index.aspx?nid=335.

36. Ibid.

37. "A Conversation with Eckhart Tolle and Deepak Chopra," filmed April 24, 2013, http://www.eckharttolletv.com.

38. Anita Moorjani, *Dying To Be Me: My Journey from Cancer, to Near Death, to True Healing* (New York: Hay House, 2012).

39. Ibid., 76.

40. Ibid., 115.

41. Jill Bolte Taylor, *My Stroke of Insight: A Brain Scientist's Personal Journey* (New York: Plume, 2009). Also see her TED Talk, filmed February 2008, http://www.ted.com/talks/jill_bolte_taylor_s_powerful_stroke_of_insight.

42. Ibid., 71.

43. Ibid., 70.

44. Luke 10:38–42.

45. *My Stroke of Insight*, 77.

46. Ibid., 126.

47. Ibid., 152.

48. Ibid., 140.

49. Ibid., 147.

50. "The Intelligent Plant," *The New Yorker*, December 16, 2013, http://www.newyorker.com/magazine/2013/12/23/the-intelligent-plant.

51. Ibid.

52. Ibid.

53. Frances Hodgson Burnett, *The Secret Garden* (New York: Barnes and Noble, 2011).

54. Ibid., 277.

55. *Dying to Be Me*, 137.

56. Headspace "Blue Sky" animation, https://www.youtube.com/watch?v=DmqI1u72QLU_-_t=31.